The opinions expressed in this book are for general information only and are not intended to provide specific advice or recommendations for any individual. To determine which investment(s) may be appropriate for you, consult your financial advisor prior to investing. All performance is historical and is no guarantee of future results. All indices are unmanaged and cannot be invested into directly.

This information is not intended to be a substitute for specific individualized tax or legal advice. You should discuss your specific situation with a qualified tax and/or legal advisor.

Table of Contents

Preface

A few words about how this book came to be. When I began my financial management practice I searched for a book I could recommend to my clients so they could better understand what I was recommending and why. I couldn't find one. I began to think the only way I was going to find the book I really wanted was to write it. The final decision came after I was at a training session for a major regional brokerage firm, where I criticized the methods they were proposing because the approach would not optimize my clients' return on their investments. The trainer replied, "You don't have time to optimize their returns. You just have to provide them with an acceptable return so you can spend your time growing your business." I couldn't have disagreed more.

This was just one example of a harsh reality: the interests of financial advisors and the interests of their clients are not always served optimally by the same strategy. This is not to imply that financial advisors are generally less than ethical. Far from it. The vast majority make an honest effort to serve their clients well. I just feel it is important for clients to understand how the investment world works so they can judge whether the portion of their return on investment that goes to advisors, managers, etc. is offset by the added value these professionals provide. My hope is that this book helps them achieve that understanding.

I came to writing this book by a long and circuitous route. Financial management is my sixth career, and each of the first five contributed something. The first career as a catholic priest gave me valuable experience in counseling. In addition, the fine men who were involved in my seminary training felt the standard curriculum might not be challenging enough to keep me out of trouble, so they urged me to add a second major in mathematics. The second career was political consultant, where I got a crash course in understanding marketing. From there I moved on to university administration and teaching organizational behavior and statistics. The organizational behavior experience helped in the fourth career, high tech sales and marketing management, which I pursued for nearly 20 years. In the middle of that period I spent two years as the VP of Sales for a company selling venture capital limited partnerships - my first foray into the world of securities. Then I tried retirement, but in 2008 some of my friends suffered serious damage to their portfolios and I wanted to help them. So I started a financial management practice.

This book is targeted to the intelligent and generally educated reader who is not trained in the esoterica of finance. My goal is to give the reader a good lay person's understanding of the issues involved in personal investing.

I will leave it to the reader to decide whether my goal has been achieved.

Introduction

What this book is

This book is as much about LIFE as it is about MONEY. It is based on a few fundamental principles:

1. **Money is a means NOT an end**. Another way to say this is that, for most of us, investment strategy should serve life goals. Examples of life goals would be having a comfortable retirement, sending kids to college, creating a charitable foundation, or having another career without income worries. This book is all about defining life goals and then developing a financial strategy to make those goals achievable.

2. The strategy chosen to work toward your goal should be the **lowest risk strategy that has a high probability of achieving the goal**. This is a subtle but important point. Investment strategy should not be about trying to make the most money possible regardless of risk. It should also not just be about attempting to minimize risk. It is about taking *only the amount of risk* that is necessary to achieve the goal, and no more. The goal is primary and the strategy follows from the goal. Please remember, no strategy assures success or guarantees protection against loss.

3. Goals and their supporting **strategies should normally stay in place for a significant period of time**. The very minimum would be five years, but twenty or thirty years or more would be more common. And the investment time horizon extends to the *end* of the goal, not the *beginning* of it. For example, if a person were fifty, intended to retire at seventy, and expected to live until ninety, the investment strategy would need to plan for 40 years not 20 years. The fact that the time horizon is 40 years has an enormous impact on the strategy.

4. **The strategy should be reviewed at least once a year**. Economic factors change, life situations change, and goals can change. These may require a change in strategy. But, in the absence of some radical change in life circumstance (like getting married or winning the lottery), you would expect to make *minor* adjustments to the strategy, not radically change it.

5. **Large swings in the stock market, such as the one we experienced in 2008-10, are a normal part of economic life.** They are not an aberration; they happen every few years.[1] A financial strategy should be designed both to help minimize the negative impacts of the swings and take advantage of the potential opportunities that the swings present.

6. **The fundamental bases of investment theory for the past 40 years have been seriously flawed.** Unfortunately, these flawed theories have caused many investors to suffer unnecessary losses during some periods of time and fail to achieve gains in other periods. We need to find new and better approaches to work towards achieving financial goals. Some of the advice in this book will be rejected by many financial advisors because they have been trained in and still believe the flawed theories. The details my critique of conventional theory are discussed in a separate chapter.

What This Book is Not

This book is not about finding ways to get extraordinary gains in a short period of time. While there are occasional good opportunities when the market misprices assets, striving for extraordinary results generally means taking extraordinary risks. Over the long haul, extraordinary risks will make the life goals less likely to be achieved.

This book is not about picking out individual investments. It is about *whole portfolios* of investments. When you are considering the addition of an investment to a portfolio or the substitution of one investment for another, you should ask yourself, "Will the new investment make the portfolio more likely to potentially meet its objective?" For example, you may feel that Exxon Mobil is a good company and would be a good investment. But if you already own stock in four other oil companies, it may not be a good fit for your portfolio.

---

[1] Mandlebrot, Benoit and Richard Hudson *The (Mis)Behavior of Markets*, Basic Books, New York, 2004 p96

This book is definitely NOT about finding the next "hot stock". If that is how you approach investing, you may want to put this book back on the shelf. If playing the market is irresistible, then you need to make a clear distinction between your "play money" and you long term serious money. The play money should be disassociated from the process of working toward life goals. Your life goals need to still be achievable even if all the play money is lost. Any gains can be treated as an unexpected bonus.

Stocks are not "pets". There is no business reason to get emotionally attached to stocks; stocks are *investments* that may help work toward achieving *financial* goals. This is serious! Investing in stocks involves risk, including loss of principal. If you prefer to take an emotional approach to investing, you will find little help here. The approach in this book is straight-forward and logical. It is about **goals** and **strategies** - not likes and dislikes.

Chapter 1: Setting Goals

If you don't know where you are going, any route will get you there.

S.M.A.R.T. Goals

You have probably heard or seen the acronym that goals should be S.M.A.R.T.:

- Specific,
- Measurable,
- Achievable,
- Relevant
- Time-bound.

Any statement of a goal should be tested to see if it has the five S.M.A.R.T characteristics. Let's take look at some retirement goals as to see how this would apply.

Goal Statement #1: I would like to be able to retire and have enough money so I would never have to worry.

Goal Statement #2: I have $300,000 now at age 50 and I would like to be able to retire at 70 with an income of $5000 per month (indexed at 2% for inflation each year after that) and have enough resources so I could live to 95 without running out of money.

See the difference? It would be very hard to build a plan around Goal Statement #1. There is no way to know how much is "enough", how to measure progress toward achieving the goal, and how to know whether the goal needs to be adjusted. Goal Statement #2 meets the S.M.A.R.T. criteria. It is very specific. A calculation can easily be done to determine how much money would be needed for the person to retire at age 70. Progress toward acquiring that sum can be measured. The statement is clearly relevant to the retirement goal. And the time frame is clearly stated. Not only could a plan be tailored to work toward the goal, but a plan could also to measure progress toward the goal at regular intervals, adjusting the plan as needed.

Let's try another example.

Goal Statement #3: I would like to send my daughter to college.

Goal Statement #4: My daughter is now 13 and I would like to be able to contribute $20,000 per year toward her college education beginning when she is 18 and lasting for 5 years.

Again, the latter goal statement is one to build a plan around; the former doesn't give you much to go on. With goal statement #4 a plan could start with the assets now available, calculate how much additional is needed, and determine a strategy for acquiring the necessary assets.

Key Questions for Setting Your Financial Goals

1. **How much money will I need to address my goal?** How do you figure this out? One way is to meet with a financial advisor who has the tools to do the analysis. If you want to do it yourself, you can search the internet for "retirement planning calculator," or "college funding calculator," or some other search phrase appropriate to your goal. You will find online resources that allow you to plug in some numbers and get estimates.

   There are two ways of looking at the amount you will need: by relying *earnings only* or by *gradually liquidating principal*. In the first, you use only your earnings (e.g. interest, dividends, partnership distributions, etc.) to address your goal. In the second, you not only use earnings but you also gradually use the principal. Your choice depends, in part, on the nature of your goal. For example, an "earnings only" strategy would be less risky in planning retirement because you can't be sure how long you will live and using the earnings only approach would mean you would not run out of money before you die. Any remainder could be left to your heirs. However, "liquidating principal" may be more appropriate for financing college because the time line is more certain and once the goal is achieved no more assets need be dedicated to it. One thing to keep in mind here is that as you reduce the principal you also reduce to ability of the principal to generate earnings.

2. **How much has already been accumulated to contribute toward achieving the goal?** Be sure to keep this money separate from your emergency fund. Most people should reserve a *minimum* of three months living expenses in an emergency fund before doing other investing, and maybe even six or nine months depending on individual situations. You would want to avoid spending your retirement money or your child's college money in an emergency.

3. **How many years do I have to accumulate the necessary funds?** Obviously, the shorter the time the larger each contribution will have to be. This is one reason why it is important to begin early so you can work towards your goals with smaller annual contributions. Starting a college savings plan when your baby is born can take a lot of the pain out of saving. Thinking about retirement in your 30's can greatly reduce your stress in your 50's. But if you are late starting, don't despair. Starting now is better than giving up.

4. **How much will I be able to continue to contribute once I begin using my nest egg?** For example, maybe you will want to get a part time job after retirement or help pay for college out of your current income while your child is in college. This reduces the amount you will have to accumulate.

5. **How much can I contribute per year, given my resources and other obligations?** The important thing is to be sure your regular contribution is *realistic*. If it isn't, you are likely to give up. If the required contribution is *not* comfortable, maybe you need to adjust

the goal. This whole process may require several repetitions until you come up with both a goal and a contribution level that you can live with. *Be realistic.* Good intentions do not make progress towards goals; actions do.

6. **What rate of return on my investments would be required to achieve the goal with my planned contributions, and is that rate of return realistic and appropriate for my risk tolerance?** Once you have determined the amount you need and the time you have, you can calculate the required rate of return using a "compound interest calculator" that you can find on the internet. But beware of a required rate of return higher than 7%. You need to keep expectations realistic because you can't expect everything to go right during your accumulation period. You can expect at least one year out of every three or four to be a negative year for your investments.

Multiple Goals Mean Complex Strategy

An overall financial and investing strategy can be fairly complex. It often involves multiple goals such as buying a house, financing college, and preparing for retirement. It also involves prioritizing those goals both for importance and for timing. So a portfolio may have multiple time horizons with different amounts of resources needed at different times. It may also have different rates of contribution during different periods of your life.

Different stages of life may require different risk management strategies. For example, insurance may be very important when children are dependent on adult earnings for support. But if your children are grown and you have accumulated enough assets to meet your obligations, insurance may become much less important. Then, later in life when tax efficient wealth transfer becomes an issue, insurance may become important again. (The death benefit of a life insurance policy is generally not taxable to the beneficiary.)

Also, you can invest retirement assets in higher risk investments earlier in life to pursue higher return because there is time to ride out the economic cycles. However, as the time for retirement gets closer, the risk level needs to be reduced for many people, because the time they want to retire may come during an economic downturn.

Before you continue with this book, take some time out and write down your goals with as much specificity as possible. That will help you keep them in mind as you develop your investment strategy.

Chapter 2: Understanding What Risk Really Means

Almost every investor has fear of losses at least in the back of his or her mind if not in the front. So let's start by developing a real understanding of what risk means.

First a hard fact: there is no risk-free approach to investing. You could follow all the suggestions in this book – or any other book on investing – and still lose money. But following sound principles to *reduce* risk is still important.

One of the core problems with conventional investing theory is with how the theories characterize and measure risk. Conventional theory tends to both underestimate risk and measure it incorrectly. Chapter 11 goes more deeply into why this has happened, but here we are going to try to get our heads around what risk really is.

Financial advisors are trained to assess a wide variety of risks. Let's look at a few ways that the performance of our investments and, therefore, the journey toward our life goals, could be impacted by different types of risk.

Types of Risk

- **Market Risk** -The risk that an entire category of investments (e.g. stocks or bonds) or a segment of the economy (e.g. financial services companies) will perform below expectations. The market crash of 2008 is an example of market risk.
- **Business or Credit Risk** – The risk that the particular entity in which we have invested (the company in which you buy stock or the issuer of bonds) will not be well managed and will fail to achieve its financial objectives. The BP oil spill and the impact on BP stock price is an example of business risk.
- **Concentration Risk** – The risk that too much of a portfolio is concentrated in a single investment or in a group of very similar investments. For example, if your portfolio had 10% each in Ford Chrysler, and General Motors, there are some periods when it

would have performed very well. But we know what would have happened in the last few years.

- **Inflation Risk** – The risk that inflation will cause the costs of your goal to be greater than what your investments produce. In the 1970's the US economy went through a period of very high inflation. Anyone on a fixed income during that period saw the purchasing power of their money severely impacted. If your investment horizon is long, it is likely that you will see at least one period of high inflation.

- **Liquidity Risk** – The risk that your investment will not be able to be sold when you need the money, forcing you to drastically reduce the price in order to sell. Real estate is an example of this. It can be a good investment, but you may not always be able to sell it quickly if you need the cash. If real estate is a major part of your investment strategy, you might want to consider balancing it with more liquid investments.

- **Longevity Risk** – In the case of retirement, it is the risk that you will run out of money before you die and be left with no resources to meet basic needs. In other words, "You want to run out of months before you run out of money." Keep in mind, a person who is 50 today and who lives to 90 will then be treated with 2050 medical techniques, which may increase the chances of living even longer.

- **Currency Risk** – The risk that the relationship of US dollars to currencies in the rest of the world may cause the price of something you need to rise to an unacceptable level. For example, with such a high proportion of US consumer goods being manufactured overseas, a fall in the value of the dollar could negatively impact consumer prices.

- **Reinvestment Risk** – The risk that an investment (usually a fixed income investment such as a bond or a CD) will mature at a time of low interest rates and the money will have to be invested at the then current lower rates. If the investor is counting on the interest for living expenses, this can be critical. Suppose you had single $100,000 bond invested at 6% interest and you were counting on the $6,000 to help with meeting your needs. Then the bond matured and you could only reinvest it at 3%. You would not have sufficient resources.

- **Interest Rate Risk** – This is, in some ways, the opposite of reinvestment risk. If interest rates go up, the market value of fixed interest rate investments, such as bonds, will go down. If maintaining *the market value* of the portfolio is more important to the investor than the absolute dollar amount of the income, then this risk is important.
- **Death or Disability Risk** – The risk that we will either die or become disabled before we can accumulate sufficient resources to achieve the goal. (Some goals, such as supporting a spouse or paying for college can continue after death.) Insurance is the primary protection against this risk.

It is important to realize that these risks interact with each other. For example, an investor who is too concerned about market risk and therefore invests too conservatively can exacerbate the inflation risk and the longevity risk. My own grandfather endured significant losses in the great depression, so he invested only in insured savings accounts. Even though he started with more than adequate resources, inflation ate up the purchasing power of his savings and he outlived his money.

Wow, that all sounds pretty scary! But there are good ways to manage these risks, which we will get to in the next chapter.

There are other ways to characterize risks such as **idiosyncratic risk** and **systemic risk**. "Idiosyncratic" is the risk that a particular investment will perform badly. "Systemic" is the risk that an entire segment of the overall financial system will perform badly. A clear example of this is what happened with mortgage backed securities in the 2008 crash. Wall Street banks constructed securities made up of home mortgages. They came up with sophisticated ways of slicing and dicing the securities to make them appear less risky than they really were. The rating agencies were fooled by these techniques and rated many of these securities AAA. However, in reducing the idiosyncratic risk (the risk that the failure of any one mortgage would impact the security), these securities actually *concentrated* the systemic risk (the risk that if one mortgage went bad the rest would also go bad).

What Makes Crashes Happen?

One of the big fears investors have, especially after 2008, is that the whole stock market will crash. In my opinion, this is one of the areas where conventional theory has been consistently wrong. Market crashes are not generally caused by market fundamentals - they are primarily caused by psychological factors – the behavior of investors individually and as a group.

As one expert has put it, "In financial markets, crashes occur because of increasing synchronizations of the market participants."[2] In other words, investors see other investors running for the exits and they join the herd.

The famous investor Sir John Templeton had a description of the causes of business cycles, "Bull markets are born in pessimism, grow in optimism, and die in euphoria." Some investors begin to believe, for whatever reason, valid or invalid, that their investments are going to lose value. So they begin to sell. The selling causes the prices to fall. Other investors see the falling prices and become fearful, so they sell too. Then prices begin to fall even more frightening even more investors and and pretty soon it's a stampede.

Intelligent portfolio management techniques can be used to help reduce the impact of crashes and potentially take advantage of the opportunities presented in the post-crash periods.

---

[2] Montier, James *Behavioral Finance, Insights into Irrational Minds and Markets*, John Wiley, West Sussex, 2002 p141

Chapter 3: Some Tools for Risk Management

There are two statistical concepts that are important in understanding how to manage risk. (If you are a bit math-phobic, don't worry; they are easy to understand.)

The Concept of Correlation

Paying attention to correlation is one way of managing risk. In statistics, correlation is a measurement of how much the changes in two sets of data - such as the value of two different investments tend to vary in the same way. The amount of similarity is expressed by the *coefficient of correlation*, a number that varies from 1 to -1. In the case of investments, a coefficient of 1 means that the two investments vary in exactly the same way - when one goes up, the other goes up; when one goes down, the other goes down too. A coefficient of -1 means they vary in exactly the opposite way - when one goes up, the other goes down. A coefficient of 0 means there is no discernible relationship in how they vary. In building a portfolio, it is important to include investments that do not have high positive correlations to keep the portfolio balanced and to prevent the entire portfolio from reacting in the same way to a set of events.

That said, there is no guarantee that diversifying a portfolio will enhance returns or that a diversified portfolio will outperform a non- diversified portfolio. Also, diversification does not provide protection against overall market risk, or, using the concept we just learned, it protects against idiosyncratic risk but not against systemic risk.

The Concept of Expected Value

Here's another way to manage the risks in a portfolio. Statistics has a concept called "Expected Value" that lets you evaluate risk by combining both the probability of an event happening with the magnitude of the gain potential or loss. It is calculated very simply by multiplying the probability that an event will happen times the outcome if it does happen. For example, if I told you to flip a coin and that, if it came up heads, I would give you $5; your expected value would be the probability of your outcome (.5) times the magnitude of the gain ($5) and your *expected value* would be $2.50. If I then asked you to pay me $1 for the chance to flip the coin and win $5, it would be an acceptable risk because your cost ($1) would be less than the expected value ($2.50).

Let's make it a little more complicated. Imagine you can pay $5 for a chance to spin an honest roulette wheel with numbers 1-100. If your number comes up you win $400. Is it an acceptable risk? No. Why? Because the expected value is $4 (.01 time 400) and your cost to take the chance is $5. This is exactly how casinos make money – *they make sure that the expected value of the payoff is less than the price to play.* In the long run they know the house will win.

In summary, risk has two dimensions: a) the probability of a loss occurring and b) the size of the loss if it does occur. Risk *management*, therefore, must also have two dimensions: 1) trying to decrease the probability that a loss will occur, and 2) trying to decrease the size of that loss if it does occur. Even a small probability that an event will occur may be unacceptable if the consequences of that event are devastating. Again, the roulette wheel can provide an example. Suppose you had to pay $1 and if it landed on any number 1-99 you won $2, but if it landed on 100 you lost $100,000. Would you play? You better not! You have 99 chances out of 100 of winning, but the benefit of winning is minimal and the cost of losing is catastrophic.

The concept of expected value is especially important when making aggressive investments. The potential gain is high, but so is the probability of failure.

These two concepts – managing correlation and the impact of expected value - are used in developing an investment portfolio by dividing the portfolio into many small investments, some of which have low correlations to others. One of the principles I rely on is to be sure that any single investment could lose all of its value (i.e. be worth nothing) without substantially impacting the value of the portfolio as a whole. In life, anything can happen. Think about it: twenty years ago who would have thought the General Motors stock would become worthless?

Chapter 4: Rules for Managing Risk

A practical, real-world approach to risk management needs to be based on assumptions that reflect how things really are. So before we get to the rules, let's list the assumptions on which those techniques are based.

Assumptions

1. Investments are inherently risky and most are more risky than the investment industry generally admits. People are scared for good reasons.
2. Some investments are more risky than others, and more risk usually, but not always, means more opportunity for gain.
3. Any investment could lose most or all of its value. It may not be likely, but it is possible.
4. Investment cycles will happen and they will happen relatively frequently. The impact of the cycles is more severe that conventional investment theory is willing to admit.
5. Every few years a market "crash" will happen. The effects of the crash can be devastating if a portfolio is not well designed and can present an opportunity to the intelligent investor.
6. It is possible for a strategy to be *too conservative* to achieve the investment goals.
7. The appropriate level of risk is the amount required to achieve the investment goals and *no more*.

Develop an Appropriate Asset Allocation Strategy

Virtually all investment strategies can be grouped under one of two broad headings; **market timing** or **asset allocation**. The two can also be blended by mostly using one and modifying it with a little of the other.

Market timing involves studying the behavior of the markets to speculate on when the price of a particular investment or class of investments will go up or down in value. The market timer attempts to buy investments when they are expected to go up soon and sell when they are expected to go down soon. This approach is popular, *but it rarely works*. The overwhelming body of evidence shows that most money managers who attempt to time the market, in the long run, fail to achieve better returns than a naïve "buy and hold" strategy.[3] In other words, they take a whole lot more risk for no apparent additional reward.

The **asset allocation** approach determines in advance the appropriate mix of classes of investments for a particular investor's goals, asset size, time horizon, and volatility tolerance (e.g. 30% domestic stocks, 20% international stocks, 30% corporate bonds, 10% muni bonds, 10% REITS). Since market conditions are always in flux, the values of the various asset categories change unequally thereby changing the proportions of each asset category in the portfolio. This is why portfolios need to be re-balanced regularly. Either at regular time periods or when the "out of balance" reaches predetermined thresholds, the portfolio is rebalanced by selling some of what has gone up and buying some of what has gone down. An interesting side effect of this approach is that it imposes a discipline of *selling high and buying low*. But even after all that work, asset allocation does not assure a profit or guarantee against a loss.

The classes of investment that can be included in an asset allocation plan are discussed in more detail later, but the core of the allocation should be the percentage allocated to **equities** [e.g. stocks, Real Estate Investment Trusts (REITs,) Master Limited Partnerships] and the percentage allocated to **fixed income** (e.g. bonds, CD's) with other categories having small percentages if appropriate.

The two strategies can be blended by varying the allocation amounts based on speculations about the short term performance of certain investment classes. The basic portfolio structure is called the **strategic allocation** and the variations in the basic plan are called **tactical allocations**. Some analysts use the terms "overweight" and "underweight" to indicate that a particular class or sector should receive more or less than its normal allocation. To use a simple example, let's say the strategic allocation for a

---

[3] Gibson, Roger Asset Allocation: Balancing Financial Risk, McGraw Hill, NY, 2008 p14

portfolio is 60% stocks and 40% bonds. The portfolio manager may feel that stocks are undervalued and may soon increase in value. So the portfolio is tactically adjusted to 65% stocks and 35% bonds by selling some bonds and buying some stocks. This approach can also be applied to sectors of the market, for example overweighting utilities and underweighting industrial companies.

Focus on Quality Investments

The core of any portfolio should be a) in the stocks of companies with a long track record of success and b) in investment grade bonds issued by reliable organizations. Please keep in mind that past performance is no guarantee of future results. Still, in many situations you should be able to address your financial goals with no more than a very small percentage of the portfolio allocated to aggressive investments. The tip from the guy at the water cooler should be viewed as entertainment, not as part of an investing strategy. As an investor with a layman's knowledge, it would be difficult for you to obtain information that would give an advantage over the professional investor, unless that information is illegal insider information. There is no free lunch. Chasing inordinately high returns almost always means taking inordinately high risks.

Don't Invest Blind

Never invest in an individual equity unless you or your financial advisor has read and understood the company's financial statements. If you are not confident that you can understand the financial statements then you need professional help. Subscribing to a stock evaluation service like S&P, Morningstar, or Value Line can be very useful, especially as an initial screen. But they are not a substitute for either doing your own research or having research done by a professional who understands your individual goals and volatility tolerance. If an advisor tells you they don't have time to understand the underlying economics of an investment they recommend, then you should find another advisor.

Allocate as Conservatively as You Can and Still Address Your Goals

There are several ways of ranking portfolios based on the aggressiveness or conservatism of their strategy. Here is typical hierarchy going form most aggressive to most conservative:

- Aggressive Equity
- All Equity
- Growth
- Balanced toward Growth
- Balanced
- Balanced toward Income
- Income
- Conservative Income (Preservation of Capital)

The farther toward the top of the list a portfolio's strategy is, the higher potential return and higher the probability of sustaining a significant loss. As the portfolio moves down the list, the potential return decreases, but so does the probability of sustaining a big loss.

An example of an Aggressive Equity portfolio would be one that consisted entirely of small capitalization and emerging market stocks. (A company's "capitalization" is the stock price multiplied by the number of shares outstanding.) The All Equity portfolio would be all stocks, mostly large capitalization companies. The Growth, Balanced Toward Growth, Balanced, and Balanced toward Income portfolios would contain increasing amounts of fixed income investments such as bonds or CD's. The Conservative Income would contain only government guaranteed securities. Government bonds and treasury bills are guaranteed by the US government as to the timely payment of principal and interest, and, if held to maturity, offer a fixed rate of return and fixed principal value.

Consistent with the principles of this book, the ideal type of portfolio for you is the most conservative type that will have a high probability of addressing your particular goals. Further, if the investor does well in the early years and a more conservative portfolio would still achieve the goals, then the investor should address either changing the goals or changing the portfolio to work toward making it more conservative.

It is important to keep in mind that while aggressive portfolios are more vulnerable to market and business risks, conservative portfolios can be more vulnerable to inflations and interest rate risks. *Balance is critical.*

Diversify, Diversify, Diversify

A portfolio should be built so that any individual investment (including funds if they are used as described in Chapter 10) should only be between one and five percent of the portfolio, depending on the size of the portfolio. If it is any higher than that, there is probably too much risk; if it is significantly lower the investor is probably sacrificing return by including less effective investments. It should be noted here that diversification is intended to reduce the probability and the magnitude of loss, it doesn't guarantee against loss.

Diversify by Investment Class

The most basic portfolio division is into equities and fixed income. However, many other types of investment can be included. See the Chapters on Portfolio Building for the other options

Diversify by Sector of the Economy

Many stock analysts divide companies into ten sectors based on the kind of business they do. The sectors are:

- industrials
- communications,
- energy
- financial services
- health care
- technology
- utilities
- materials

- consumer staples
- consumer discretionary.

Some analysts divide these sectors into subsectors. For example, health care might be divided into hospital companies, pharmaceutical companies, and medical equipment companies. Of course, some companies do business in more than one of these sectors or subsectors, but the analysts will label them with the one that seems most appropriate. A well designed portfolio will include the stocks of companies in most, if not all, of the sectors. Things can happen in the general economy that adversely impact a particular sector, so you don't want to be overly vulnerable to the decline of any one sector. For example, a rise in oil prices would negatively impact airline stocks and positively impact oil company stocks, whereas a fall in oil prices would have the opposite effect. If both are in your portfolio you are more protected against this impact.

Many financial advisors and brokerage portfolio models follow a standard approach to diversifying by sector is by having your portfolio replicate the proportions in the Standard & Poor (S&P) 500 Index. (The S&P 500 Index is a capitalization weighted index of 500 stocks designed to measure the broad performance of the domestic economy through changes in the aggregate market value of 500 stocks representing all major industries. The Index is unmanaged and cannot be invested in directly.) In my opinion this doesn't make a lot of sense. If you are going to do that, why not just buy an S&P 500 Index fund? The sector weightings should depend on your goal and how much aggressiveness is required to work toward your goal.

For example, if you are 30 years old and you have a good income and a pretty high volatility tolerance you may want to have a higher proportion of technology stocks in your portfolio to try for higher growth, On the other hand, if you are 55, you don't have a lot of income to spare, and you are starting to worry about retirement you might want to have a higher proportion of dividend paying utility stocks. Back to our first principle – the investment strategy needs to be driven by the goals you are trying to achieve. Never allow yourself to be put into anyone's cookie cutter strategy.

Diversify by Geography

The core of most portfolios consists of stocks and bonds from the United States, the European Union, and Japan, because these are the most developed areas with the longest track records of performance. A component could be added from the so-called BRIC countries, Brazil, Russia, India, and China, because these are countries that are developing faster than the core and are in the process of moving from emerging markets to developed markets. A small component could be added from emerging market areas such as South America, Eastern Europe, and Southeast Asia. Such diversification allows you to participate in potential gains in particular geographies without being in too much danger of large losses. Remember again, diversification is a good technique, but it does not guarantee either making a profit or avoiding losses.

Diversify by Individual Investment

No individual investment (stock, bond, Real Estate Investment Trust ((REIT)), etc.) should be more than 5% of a portfolio. In a well-designed portfolio, any one investment could then become completely worthless (an unlikely event if they are well selected) without severely damaging the overall portfolio. No matter how strong a company seems, things can happen. Remember Enron and Worldcom?

Dividends Matter

For the S&P 500 companies, going all the way back to 1870, the impact of dividends has made up slightly more than half of the total return when compared to capital appreciation alone.[4] Capital appreciation is the gain from an increase in the stock price.

Paying attention to current yield can help manage risk. The "current yield" [5]of a portfolio consists of dividends, interest, and distributions from

---

[4] Wilson, Jack W. and Charles P. Jones, "An Analysis of the S&P 500 Index and Cowles Extensions: Price Indexes and Stock Returns, 1870-1999, Journal of Business, Vol. 25, No. 3, 2002
[5] Current yield is calculated by dividing the actual annual interest or dividend payments by the current market value.

RIET's and partnerships that are not return of capital. Total return consists of the combination of current yield and capital appreciation (the increase in the value of the assets in your portfolio). The key is to balance these two components to optimize total return at your acceptable level of risk. Of course, it is possible for the capital appreciation to be negative. If capital appreciation is positive (i.e. the stock prices went up), current yield increases the total return even more; if capital appreciation is negative (i.e. the stock prices went down), current yield helps reduce the negative impact.

The following table illustrates how current yield affects the amount of capital appreciation necessary to achieve a 6% total return. The columns in the table indicate what percentage of the portfolio is in equities, with the assumption that the remainder is fixed income. The rows show the current yield (income from interest, dividends, Limited Partnership distributions, etc.) as a percent of the whole portfolio value. The percentages in the table show how much the equity portion of the portfolio would have to appreciate to achieve a 6% total return at that level of current yield. So, for example, if a portfolio had 60% equities and the current yield (interest, dividends, etc.) were 4%, you look at the intersection of the 60% equity column and the 4% current yield row. The equity part of the portfolio would only have to appreciate 3.33% in capital gains to achieve a 6% total return. At a 5% current yield, the required capital gain on the equities drops to 1.67%.

The table doesn't attempt to predict outcomes, it just illustrates a mathematical concept. Two other factors need to be remembered here:

- First, the value of the fixed income part of the portfolio also changes in value. To the extent that it declines, there would be an offset to any gains in the equity part of the portfolio.
- Second, it is possible that the changes in value of both the equity and fixed income parts of the portfolio could be negative.

Current yield %	% Equities									
	70	65	60	55	50	45	40	35	30	25
1.0	7%	8%	8%	9%	10%	11%	13%	14%	17%	20%
1.5	6%	7%	8%	8%	9%	10%	11%	13%	15%	18%
2.0	6%	6%	7%	7%	8%	9%	10%	11%	13%	16%
2.5	5%	5%	6%	6%	7%	8%	9%	10%	12%	14%
3.0	4%	5%	5%	5%	6%	7%	8%	9%	10%	12%
3.5	4%	4%	4%	5%	5%	6%	6%	7%	8%	10%
4.0	3%	3%	3%	4%	4%	4%	5%	6%	7%	8%
4.5	2%	2%	3%	3%	3%	3%	4%	4%	5%	6%
5.0	1%	2%	2%	2%	2%	2%	3%	3%	3%	4%
5.5	1%	1%	1%	1%	1%	1%	1%	1%	2%	2%
6.0	0%	0%	0%	0%	0%	0%	0%	0%	0%	0%

Assuming value of fixed come assets remained constant, how would the equity portion have to grow to achieve a 6% yield in the overall portfolio

Don't Chase Yields at the Expense of Quality

While dividends are very important, they are not the only factor involved in selecting an investment. There are many reasons why dividend yield can be high, most good but some bad. Since yield is calculated by dividing the amount of the dividend by the stock price, one reason for high yield could be that the stock price has dropped. Is this a red flag or an opportunity? It depends.

With high dividend stocks it is really important to study the company's financial statements to be sure the dividend is sustainable. Of course basic analysis of revenue trends, profit trends, and competitive positioning are important. But beyond that you should look at the "payout ratio". This is the percentage of earnings that is paid out in dividends. Anything above 75% is cause for further analysis.

If you subscribe to an analytical service, as you should if you are managing your own portfolio, one of the metrics you will see is "free cash flow". Free cash flow can sometimes be significantly higher than earnings. If so, one place to look for the cause is in the difference between depreciation and capital expenditures. Depreciation is an amount a company subtracts from its revenues in calculating earnings. (Depreciation is this year's allocation of what was paid for capital equipment in past years; capital expenditures is the amount the company is spending on capital equipment this year.) In this case it is important to calculate dividends as a percentage of free cash flow. Most of the analytical services don't report this, but it is easy to calculate. The simple formula is: multiply the annual dividend amount by the number of shares outstanding and divide that by the free cash flow. This needs to be below the 75% level.

Try to Meet Retirement Goals Using Only Current Yield

Simple fact: you have no idea how long you are going to live.

Once you retire you are going to begin spending your assets using one of two methods. One method is to gradually spend the principal and hope that the money won't run out before you die. The other is to use the interest and dividends and avoid touching the principal.

Let's look at an example that shows why there can be a big difference between these methods. It's a little oversimplified, but it illustrates the point. A 65-year old investor retired in 2006 with $1,000,000 and is selling enough assets to get $40,000 a year while still adding 2% each year for inflation. Since the long term return on her portfolio was expected to be 7% and she was selling 4% per year, she felt comfortable that she would not outlive her money. Then 2008 came along and her assets lost 50% of their value. Now they are only worth $500,000. She has to spend 8% of her assets to maintain her lifestyle during the year of the recession. Now she only has $460,000. From this point on, her portfolio will have to average more than 10% for her to meet her goal. The risk required to reach that aggressive of a goal puts her in even greater danger of suffering another major loss.

Let's look at an alternative scenario in which the investor only had to rely on current yield during that same volatile period. If the portfolio had been designed to deliver a 5% current yield (a realistic goal), $40,000 could have been taken for income and the other $10,000 reinvested to address the inflation protection goal.

A real situation would, of course, be a bit more complicated because the market does not vary uniformly and the tax effects would have to be factored in, but the example illustrates the concept.

Chapter 5: Portfolio Building Blocks – Individual Investments

What is an investment?

Every investment is essentially the purchase of a future cash flow. Pay money now so that more money will be paid back later. This is the fundamental structure of any business activity – cash flow out now in the expectation of greater cash flow in later. In general, the more risk the investor is willing to take, the higher the potential return – but also, the higher the potential loss.

Our goal here is to develop a custom portfolio of investments that will give a high probability of achieving the life goals that you have established. That portfolio will be made up of a set of specific investments. What are the investment options for your portfolio? Let's go through some of the common investments, roughly in ascending order of risk/reward. The following list is by no means exhaustive and only the most common types of investments are considered.

The two major categories of investment are Fixed Income and Equities, sometimes referred to as "loan" and "own." Fixed income investments are loans made to a government, a company, or a bank to receive an interest payment. Equities involve actually owning a part of a company, trust or partnership.

The prices on fixed income investments vary inversely with interest rates. Here is an example: Suppose I make a loan of $10,000 at 5% when that is the market rate. I would be paid $500 a year in interest. Then suppose the market rate changes to 6%. A person I am selling that loan would expect to receive $600 interest on a $10,000 loan, but mine is only paying $500. So the price of the loan changes. If they bought my $10,000 loan for $8,333 they would be receiving the market rate of 6%. On the other hand, suppose the market rate dropped to 4%. They would only expect $400 in interest. So if they bought my loan for $12,500 they would be getting the 4% market rate.

Types of investments

United States Treasury Bills, Notes, and Bonds

These are securities issued directly by the United States Government. Securities with terms less than one year are called "Bills"; one to 10 years, "Notes"; and above 10 years, "Bonds". U.S. Government securities are generally considered the closest thing to a risk free security, at least from the perspective of worrying about loss of principal. A variation is Treasury Inflation Protected Securities (TIPS), a U.S. treasury investment that also offers inflation protection. TIPS are subject to market risk and significant interest rate risk because their longer duration makes them more sensitive to the price declines associated with higher interest rates. Government bills, notes and bonds are guaranteed by the US government as to timely payment of principal and interest, and if held to maturities offer a fixed rate of return and fixed principal value.

Insured Savings Accounts

Savings accounts in qualified banks and savings institutions are insured by agencies of the federal government up to a legal maximum. These accounts generally pay the lowest rates of interest, but the money is available to the depositor at any time with no withdrawal penalty. (This is the appropriate place for a family's *emergency funds*. In very low interest rate environments, people may be tempted to look for riskier investments that get higher returns. However, the federal guarantees and the immediate availability are important.)

Insured Certificates of Deposit (CD's)

CD's are like savings accounts and, at qualified institutions, can also be federally insured. The depositor agrees to allow the bank to keep the money for a defined period of time, and, in return, the bank pays a higher rate of interest than it pays on a savings account. The rate generally increases as the term gets longer. Some CD's require a minimum investment. Also, if the depositor needs the money before the CD matures, the bank charges a penalty for early withdrawal. One way to shorten the effective maturities of CD's is to "ladder" them. For example, if an investor has $30,000 to invest, $10,000 can be invested in a 30 day CD, $10,000 in a 60 day CD, and $10,000 in a 90 day CD. As each CD matures it is reinvested at the 90 day rate. That way the investor can get the 90 day rate on the new CD and still have a CD maturing every month. Obviously, this technique can also be used for longer periods.[6]

GNMA Pass-through Certificates

This investment is not as well known to the general public, but has some features that may make it interesting to some investors. The Government National Mortgage Association (GNMA also called "Ginnie Mae") collects pools of GNMA qualifying mortgages and sells shares of the pool to investors. That means that each investor owns a piece of each underlying mortgage. The timely payment of principal and interest is fully guaranteed by the full faith and credit of the United States Government. The investor receives a payment every month, passing through both the interest and the principal paid by the families who took out the mortgages. It is important to be aware that a portion of the GNMA check you receive each month is a return of your principal. If you spend it all and do not reinvest the part that is return of principle, you are depleting your assets. This may be perfectly ok, but you need to be aware you are doing it. Also, even though the payment of interest and principal is guaranteed, the yield is not and the market value can fluctuate with interest rates. This means that there could be loss of principal if the certificate is sold before all the mortgages have been repaid.

Bonds

A bond is a debt. When you buy a bond you are lending money to the bond issuer, and the bond issuer pays you interest while it uses your money and then returns your principle when the bond matures. In evaluating a bond for purchase the following considerations are important:

- **Face Value** – This is the nominal value of the bond. Minimum investment for bonds is usually $5000 and increments above the

---

[6]When the original 30 day CD matures, the original 60 day CD is 30 days from maturity and the original 90 day CD is 60 day s from maturity. The new CD is 90 days, so the maturities stay at 30, 60, and 90 days.

minimum are usually $1000 to $5000. Some brokerage firms have a $10,000 minimum. Some bonds may have much higher minimums such as $250,000.

- **Coupon Rate** – This is the amount on the face of the bond, i.e. the interest rate that was intended to be paid when the bond was originally issued.
- **Price** – This is what the investor pays for the bond. Bond prices are given in percents without the percent sign. If the price is above 100, the bond is being sold at a premium; if it is below 100, it is being sold at a discount. Since the coupon rate stays constant, the purpose of the price is to adjust the real rate of return to reflect current market conditions. So if a bond is priced at 101 and the investor is buying a $10,000 bond, it will cost $10,100; or if it is priced at 98.5, it would cost $9850. Bonds also have wholesale and retail prices. You buy the bond from a broker at the retail price, but if you sell it back the broker will pay you the wholesale price. The *spread* between the retail and wholesale price is usually 1%-2.5%. In general, the prices of bonds go down when interest rates go up and the prices go up when interest rates go down.
- **Call Provisions** – Some issuers reserve the right to pay off the bond early at specific dates in the future. When they do this they are said to "call" the bond. If a bond is called early, the yield to the investor could be affected. Sometimes bonds will pay a slight premium if they are called.
- **Yield** - This is the rate that the investor actually earns on the investment in the bond. The yield on a bond can be calculated three ways: **current yield, yield to maturity, and yield to call** (if the bond is callable). The **current yield** is calculated by dividing the actual annual interest payments by the current market value. Thus, for bonds selling at a discount, the current yield is higher than the coupon rate, and for bonds bought at a premium, the current yield is lower than the coupon rate. **Yield to maturity** is the rate an investor will earn if he holds the bond until it matures, collects all the interest payments, and is paid back the principal at maturity. Since the issuer always pays face value at maturity, the investor will receive more than the original investment if the bond was purchased at a discount and less than the original investment if

the bond was purchased at a premium. This difference is factored into the yield to maturity. **Yield to call** is the rate the investor will have earned if the issuer calls the bond at the earliest call date. The last yield concept is **yield to worst**. This is the lowest of the other three yield calculations and is how a bond should be quoted to a prospective investor.

- **Maturity** – This is the date when all of the interest will have been paid and principal is returned to the investor.
- **Duration** – This is a calculation that tells the investor when the discounted cash flow from the bond (interest and/or principle) will have equaled the original investment. It is one way of evaluating risk. We won't go into discounted cash flow because it gets pretty complicated, but you can look it up on the internet if you are interested.
- **Quality** – The quality of a bond is the estimated likelihood that all of the interest and principal payments will be made on schedule. It is usually expressed by a rating from a bond rating company. (See below.)

Municipal Bonds (Tax-free and Taxable)

Municipal Bonds or "Munis" are issued by state and local governments. Some are federal tax-free, and some are both federal and state tax free, depending on state laws. The most common types are General Obligation (GO) Bonds and Revenue Bonds. GO bonds are backed by the taxing power of the local or state government and by a commitment to tax sufficiently to be able to pay the principle and interest when due. Revenue Bonds are backed by the revenue from a particular project such as an airport or a toll bridge. The project must generate sufficient revenue to make the payments. GO bonds are generally considered lower risk than Revenue Bonds because they are backed by the taxing authority of the issuing agency, not by revenue from a specific project. (More on bond rating shortly.)

Corporate Bonds

Bonds can also be issued by private companies. Essentially, companies raise capital in two ways, by selling shares in the company (stock) or by borrowing (bonds).   Principal and interest payments depend on the company running a successful business and generating enough profit to meet its financial obligations.   Historic default rates of corporate bonds have been higher than those of municipal bonds for equivalent ratings.

Like stocks, *it is important to diversify a portfolio of bonds* by the economic sector of the issuer so the portfolio is not overly vulnerable to economic events. For example, it would not be good to have a portfolio of bonds that were all issued by financial services companies

(A note on bond ratings)

The bad thing that can happen with a bond is a *default*. Default can mean anything from a late interest payment to total loss of principal. There are three private companies, (Standard and Poor, Moody's, and Fitch) called "rating agencies", that use mathematical models to predict the probability that a default will occur and, if it does occur, how severe it will be. Based on the results of the models, the rating agencies assign a rating to a bond.

Risks in bonds

The possibility of default is, of course, one part of the risk.   But a circumstance could arise in which the bond has to be sold before maturity. The sale value of bonds generally varies inversely with changes in interest rates, i.e. if interest rates go up, bond prices go down and vice versa. The longer the maturity the more the price of the bond tends to be affected by interest rate changes.

"Laddering" Bonds

One way of managing the risk of changes in the sale price of bonds is to organize the maturities of the bonds in the portfolio so that some are short-term (less than five years), some are intermediate-term (five to fifteen years), and some are long-term (more than fifteen years). This is call laddering.

Zero Coupon Bonds

Some bonds do not have periodic payments. The total amount of the interest paid during the life of the bond is calculated and subtracted from the amount to be paid to the investor at maturity. This is the selling price of a zero coupon bond. This can be a good investment when the resources for the goal will be needed at a specific time in the future such as college education.

Preferred Stock

Preferred stock is a little bit like common stock and a little bit like a bond. The preferred stockholders receive a dividend that must be paid before any dividends are paid to common stock holders, but they generally have no voting rights. Also, if the company were to be liquidated, preferred claims rank between bondholders and common stockholders. Sometimes preferred stock is convertible to common stock under terms defined in the stock offering.

Common Stock

As mentioned above, companies can raise capital by selling shares of the company to investors. If the company succeeds and grows, theoretically the company will be worth more and that means each share will be worth more. This growth in value is called "capital appreciation." In addition, many mature companies also pay dividends, i.e. they distribute part of their earnings to shareholders on a per share basis. The combination of dividends and capital appreciation is called "total return."

Ways to categorize stocks

The most common categorization of stocks is by **the size of the companies**. This is measured by "market capitalization" which is the combined value of all the stock the company has outstanding. Large Cap companies have a market cap of $10 billion or more; mid-caps have $1 billion to $10 billion; and small caps have less than $1 billion.

Another way of categorizing is by **investment style**. The most common styles are "value," and "growth." Value investors attempt to find companies that the market is currently undervaluing. Their theory is that, eventually, the market will realize that the company is undervalued and the price of the stock will go up. Growth investors focus on companies they believe can grow their revenues and profits.

The way some analysts determine whether a stock is growth or value is to simply take an index, such as the S&P 500 or the Russell 1000, and rank the stocks by the ratio of market capitalization (the total value, based on the share price, of all the company's stock) to the book value (the value of the company's assets if they were sold off). The companies in the top half are called "growth" and the companies in the bottom half are called "value".

Another important characteristic of a stock is whether or not it **pays a dividend**, and, if so, how much.

Some important things to look for in company financial statements

Companies whose stock is listed on a stock exchange for sale to the public are required to issue accurate financial reports quarterly and to quickly make public any news that might have a "material" effect on the stock price. While materiality can be subjective, good companies would generally rather err on the side of transparency to avoid legal problems. These reports and press releases are easily available on the company's web site. The websites usually have an "Investor Relations" tab that links to a page with the key information.

> Here are a few questions to ask in reviewing the financial statements:
> - Is the company profitable?
> - Have the profits been consistent and can fluctuations be explained by fluctuations in the general economy?
> - Does the company have enough cash on its balance sheet to allow it to weather difficult times?
> - What is the ratio of current assets to current liabilities? A ratio of less than one (i.e. liabilities are higher than assets) may be a warning sign.

- If dividends are part of the reason for buying the stock, what is the track record of paying dividends? Did dividends continue during tough times? Has the dividend increased over time? What is the total dividend payout both as a percentage of earnings and as a percentage of free cash flow? Do the percentages imply that the dividend payments are sustainable?
- What is the relationship between depreciation (writing off prior investments) and capital expenditures (making new investments)? When capital expenditures are significantly lower than depreciation, additional free cash flow is created. When capital expenditures are significantly higher than depreciation it means the company has a strategy of investing for faster growth.

Real Estate Investment Trusts (REIT's)

Exchange traded REIT's hold title to real estate and similar assets and pass through the proceeds from their operations to their investors in the form of dividends. As long as a REIT passes through at least 90% of its proceeds to investors, it has what is called "conduit" status meaning that the earnings of the REIT are not taxable like the earnings of a corporation. The tax liability is passed through to the investors. This means that investors in REIT's need to be aware *that the income is "pre-tax" and should set aside the money to pay the taxes* when they come due. (Dividends in corporations could actually be taxed twice, first as corporate earnings and then as individual income for the shareholders. If they have already been taxed at the corporate level, the dividends can be "qualified" and receive a more favorable tax rate.)

Some REIT's are not traded on a major stock exchange and selling them requires finding a willing buyer. These non-exchange traded REIT's involve additional liquidity risk and may not be suitable for all investors.

Limited Partnership Units

Corporations can sell common stock. But some businesses are organized as "partnerships" rather than as corporations. The typical investment partnership has two classes of partners: the General Partner (GP) and the Limited Partners (LP's). The GP manages the business and takes all of the non-investment risks. The LP's provide the capital but take no part in the management of the company; and the LP's maximum risk is limited (hence the name) to the loss of their invested capital. Like REIT's, Limited Partnerships are not taxed; the tax liability is passed through to the partners. At the end of each year each limited partner receives a K1 form from the general partner detailing the gains or losses to be included in the limited partner's tax return. Limited partnerships are subject to special risks such as potential illiquidity and may not be suitable for all investors.

Chapter 6: Portfolio Building Blocks - Funds

All of the investments discussed so far would be considered individual investments, i.e. investments in a single instrument or organization. There is another way investments can be structured. Any combination of the investments we have listed (plus some others we haven't) can be combined into a Fund or Unit Trust. Here are the most common types of investment "baskets."

Actively Managed Mutual Funds

In these funds a set of rules is established in the fund's prospectus outlining the fund's objectives, the types of investments that can be included in the fund, and any restrictions that are put on the fund's managers. A manager (or group of managers) selects the investments for the fund, constantly monitors the performance of the investments, and moves investments into and out of the funds, attempting to maximize the total return while working within the rules established for the fund. There are more than 12,000 actively managed mutual funds operating today, specializing in all kinds of different types of investments and with many different investment strategies. Funds may specialize in companies of a particular industry, particular geography, particular size, or have a host of other characteristics. Investing in mutual funds involves risk including potential loss of principal.

Most Funds have sales charges, and virtually all have ongoing expenses. The sales charges on typical funds vary based on the fund and the size of the investment. (The mutual fund companies usually give volume discounts.) If the fund has a sales charge, it can be paid in two ways, either all up front or over time with a higher annual fee. If the sales charge is paid up front, the shares are usually called "A-shares." If the sales charge is paid over time, the shares are called "B-shares or C-Shares." A typical sales charge for mutual funds would run from 5.75% for investments of less than $25,000 to zero for investments of more than $1 million. Funds from the same mutual fund company can usually be combined to qualify for the volume discount.

The ongoing fees can range from .5% to 2%, or even higher for funds that are harder to manage. Annual fees have two components, the management fee and the "12b1 fee." The **management fee** is what the fund manager gets paid to manage the investments. The **12b1 fee** offsets marketing and servicing costs. Brokers and financial advisors generally get a portion of the 12b1 fee. They call this fee share their "trail." In a large financial advising practice, this can add up to a significant amount of money.

The investor needs to look at ALL the costs and determine whether the manager is good enough to provide an adequate return net of expenses. Note: *It's not the amount of expenses that matter, it's how much you make after the expenses are deducted.*

Whether Actively Managed Funds can consistently do well enough to justify their expenses is a controversial issue in the investing world. Professors Eugene Fama of the University of Chicago (the same one who developed the Efficient Market Hypothesis that will be discussed in a later chapter) and Kenneth French of Dartmouth say that their work shows that, on the whole, "returns realized by investors is negative by about the amount of the fund expenses."[7] That would mean that the fund managers barely made their expenses and you got nothing for taking the extra risk. Others say that they can point to particular managers who have consistently outperformed the market. The nay-sayers counter that the few that outperform is no more than one would expect from a random distribution. We will not settle the argument here.

In his classic book, *The Intelligent Investor*[8], Benjamin Graham (Warren Buffet's mentor) analyzed the results for 1969 and 1970 of the largest fund offered by each of ten management companies. In 1969 only three of these 10 funds performed better than the S&P 500 Index; in 1970 only one performed better and only by .1%. For the ten years 1961 to 1970, five of

---

[7] Journal of Finance, Vol. LXV, No. 5, p.1915

[8] Graham, Benjamin, *The Intelligent Investor*, Harper & Row, New York, 1973

the funds performed better and five performed worse. For the ones that performed better, was it skill or luck? The experts argue about that.

Passive Index Mutual Funds

For those who believe that actively managed funds are unlikely to outperform the market, there is an alternative. A fund can be structured so that it mimics the behavior of a common index such as the Dow Jones Industrial Average, the S&P 500 Index, or the New York Stock Exchange (NYSE) listed stocks. Since only minimal management is required (adjusting the "basket" when the index changes so it continues to reflect the index), the fees can be much lower. Fees for a typical S&P 500 Index fund can run .25% or even less.

Closed End Funds and Exchange Traded Funds (ETF's)

Both actively managed and passive index funds are open-ended, which means as more investors buy in to the fund, the fund simply expands by buying more investments. The alternative is a Closed End Fund where the basket of underlying investments is fixed. Once the fund is fully sold, you can only buy in by buying from someone who already owns it. If the fund offers its shares on a public exchange, such as the NYSE, it is called an Exchange Traded Fund. ETF's are frequently used to focus on a particular economic sector or geography. They trade just like stocks and their value goes up and down just like stocks. The value of the ETF is based on the cumulative value of the investments held in the fund. An investment in an Exchange Traded Fund, structured as a mutual fund or unit investment trust, involves risk of losing money and should be considered as *part* of an overall program, not a complete investment program in and of itself. Depending on their contents, investments in ETF's can also involve additional risks such as lack of diversification, price volatility, competitive industry pressure, international political and economic developments, possible trading halts, and index tracking errors.

Unit Investment Trusts (UIT's)

A UIT has a specified life. At some point in time, the trust expires and the assets are liquidated and proceeds distributed to the holders. UIT's are often used to hold a diversified portfolio of bonds, but they can be used to hold any kind of security. Unless the expiration date of the trust is directly tied to the investment objective, investors should consider both the reinvestment risks and tax consequences of investing in subsequent trusts.

Ways of Categorizing Funds

Stock Funds

The primary way that stock mutual funds are categorized is by the size of the companies they invest in and whether the investments are primarily growth stocks, value stocks, or a blend of the two. Thus, there would be names like XYZ Small-cap Value Fund, or ABC Large-cap Growth Fund. Investing in mutual funds involves risk including possible loss of principal. The prices of small cap stocks are generally more volatile than those of large cap stocks.

In addition, funds may specialize in particular geographies. A fund might invest primarily in companies in a region, such as Asia or Europe; in a specific country, such as China; or in a group of countries with a common characteristic, such as the BRIC countries (Brazil, Russia, India and China). International and emerging market investing involves additional risk such as currency fluctuations and political instability, so it may not be appropriate for all investors.

A fund might also specialize in a particular economic sector like utilities or technology. They may even specialize in a sub-sector like computer software, a sub-sector of technology, or regional banks, a subsector of financial services. Allocating assets to sectors may involve a greater degree of risk than investments with broader diversification and may limit your options.

Bond Funds

Bond funds are generally categorized by three sets of criteria.

- municipal bonds or corporate bonds;
- investment grade or high yield;
- short, intermediate, or long term maturities.

Short term is five years or less, intermediate is five to fifteen years, and long term is more than fifteen years. Similar to stock funds, the bond funds will combine these categories, so there will be names like "intermediate, investment grade, corporate bond fund" or "short duration, high yield, municipal fund."

An increase in interest rates may cause the price of bonds and bond mutual funds to decline.

Municipal bonds are subject to availability and change in price. They are subject to market and interest rate risk if sold prior to maturity. Bond values will decline as interest rates rise. Interest income may be subject to the alternative minimum tax. Municipal bonds are federally tax-free, but other state and local taxes may apply.

The market value of corporate bonds will fluctuate, and, if the bond is sold prior to maturity, the investor's yield may differ from the advertised yield.

High yield ("junk") bonds (grade BB or below) are not investment grade securities and are subject to higher interest rate, credit, and liquidity risks than those graded BBB and above. They should generally be part of a diversified portfolio for sophisticated investors

Balanced Funds

Balanced funds contain both equity and fixed income investments. The percentages of each vary according to the objective of the fund. The prospectus for the fund lays out the rules the fund manager must follow in varying the percentages.

Target Date Funds

Increasingly popular investments for retirement or college saving are **target date funds**. These are usually "funds of funds," meaning their investments are primarily in other mutual funds. The target date is the approximate date when the investors plan to start withdrawing their money. They are designed to be more aggressive when the target date for retirement or college is well out in the future and to become gradually more conservative as the target date becomes closer. For example, a target date fund may start out with a high percentage of equity funds, even including some small cap and emerging market funds. As the goal gets closer, the more aggressive parts of the fund will be traded for some fixed income. By the time the goal is imminent, the target date fund may be mostly fixed income. The principal value of a target fund is not guaranteed at any time, including at the target date.

Funds and Taxes

Tax efficiency will be dealt with in another chapter. However, one caution for the funds investor is that funds can generate tax liability without providing the cash to pay the taxes. This is sometimes called "phantom income." If the fund manager reinvests dividends or sells securities for a gain and reinvests the money, the income is taxable and the tax consequences are passed on to the fund shareholders. If there is no distribution from the fund to the shareholders, the investor will have to find other resources to pay the taxes. This is not necessarily a bad thing, but it can be if you were not expecting it and got a surprise.

Chapter 7: Portfolio Building Blocks: "Alternative Investments"

The category of alternative investments means investments other than the standard fare of stocks, bonds and mutual funds. Among the types of investment included are private equity, venture capital, hedge funds, commodities, and derivatives.

There is a simple rule for alternative investments for the average individual investor: **don't invest any money in them that you can't afford to lose**.

Private Equity

Some companies are not able to obtain the money they need to operate from standard bank credit. There can be any one of a number of reasons for this such as past credit problems, the company not having a long enough track record, or tight credit environments. Companies in this position will often go to non-bank organizations which provide credit when banks won't. Generally these loans are viewed as higher risk and therefore can demand higher returns. The skill of the private equity manager is to evaluate the creditworthiness of a prospective client, take appropriate risks, and require appropriate returns.

Sometimes private equity firms take stock in their customer companies as well as charging interest. The stock participation is most often in the form of preferred stock or warrants to buy stock at a predetermined price. The returns from this can be substantial when and if the investment is successful.

Venture Capital

Venture capital is a special kind of private equity that provides financing for start-up companies. The most famous segment of the venture capital community is located in "Silicon Valley." Venture capitalists take equity in the companies they finance in the hope that they can "exit" their investments either by selling the company's stock to the public in an initial public offering (IPO) or by selling the company to a larger company. Most venture capital investments are failures, but the few that are successful can be very successful, yielding the venture investors many times their original investment. The skill of the venture capitalists lies in managing the "bets" they make well enough so the high returns from the few successes more than offset the losses from the many failures.

Venture capital funds are usually raised from large institutions such as insurance companies and pension funds. These investors know that, in the mathematics of portfolios, if the aggressive investment is restricted to a very small percentage of the portfolio, a failure will have minimal effect on the overall result while a success can impact the results significantly.

Venture funds generally take preferred stock in the companies they support. The employees get common stock. If the company succeeds, everyone makes money. But if the company does not succeed or is sold for less than the total investment, the preferred stockholders have liquidation preference, so they divide the proceeds and the common stock is worth nothing.

Hedge Funds

The name comes from the phrase "hedging one's bets." Both business managers and investors can take investment positions that involve known risks. For example, an American company may sign a contract to deliver its products to a company in Japan at a set price over a six month period and be paid in Japanese yen. This could involve currency risk, the risk that the relative values of the US dollar and the Japanese yen could adversely affect the company's profits. The company could "hedge" that risk by buying currency future derivatives that would be profitable if the values of the currency changed in an unfavorable direction. The profit on the hedge could then help offset the loss on the exchange rate. It's a little like an insurance policy.

Since there is a market for hedge products like the one described above, fund managers can raise money from sophisticated investors to offer products to investors and corporate finance managers who are trying to hedge risks. With the increased use of computers, the products offered by these funds have become extremely complex, challenging the ability of even the most experienced investors to fully understand them.

The expenses for hedge funds can be fairly high. The so called "two and twenty" funds charge 2% of the investment and take a 20% share of the profits. With those kinds of charges the funds have to be extremely profitable to outperform standard investments, so the fund managers have to take higher risks.

Hedge funds involve special considerations and risks beyond those involved in traditional mutual funds and similar investments. Each fund is speculative and, in addition to the risks inherent in investing in any security, they can add risks associated with the use of leverage, short-sales, options, futures, derivatives, "junk bonds", non-US securities, and illiquid investments. They also have limited regulatory oversight.

Commodities

Almost all of the investments discussed in this book are financial instruments – stocks, bonds, etc. An alternative to financial instruments is to own real things such as gold, oil, cotton, or corn. These are called commodities. The investor does not usually take physical delivery of the commodities; the commodity stays in a professional storage facility and the investor just takes ownership. Fast price swings in commodities and currencies can result in significant volatility in an investor's holdings.

Commodities are traded on commodity exchanges such as the Chicago Mercantile Exchange (CME) or the New York Mercantile Exchange (NYMEX).

Derivatives

The fundamental definition of a derivative is a security whose value is based on the price or the price changes of something other than itself. Here's an example: agricultural futures. A farmer who is planting his wheat in the spring has no certainty about what the price of wheat in the fall will be. So he goes to an investor who contracts to buy his wheat at $6 a bushel at harvest time, thus giving the farmer certainty. This contract then becomes a tradable security. The value of the future contract varies based on the price of wheat. If the price of wheat drops below $6, the value of the contract goes to zero, because no investor would buy the wheat at $6 so he could sell it for less. If the price goes to $7, the future contract has a potential profit of $1 per bushel, so the value of the futures contract will go up.

The market for derivatives has exploded in recent years. One can buy derivatives based currency exchange rates, interest rates, stock indexes, and a plethora of other things. The thing on which the derivative price is based is called "the underlying."

One derivative you may have read about in the news and which is key to both the 2008 crash and the Greek debt problem is "Credit Default Swaps". They are a lot like insurance. The holders of bonds and other debt obligations pay a fee to the swap seller. The holder of the swap was entitled to payments if the defaults on the underlying securities exceeded the amount agreed upon in the contract. When the housing market began to collapse and people began to default on their mortgages, the swap holders demanded their payments. In some cases the swap sellers had believed the likelihood of default was so remote that they had not reserved funds to make payments if defaults occurred. The result was chaos in the entire financial system.

Real Estate

One very popular investment is rental real estate. The investor hopes to make money both from rents and from appreciation in the value of the property. Since most people understand this investment fairly well, we won't go into it here except to point out a couple of cautionary considerations. The first is that real estate can be relatively illiquid. If you end up in a position where you need cash, it can take months to sell a piece of real estate. The second is that rental real estate can sometimes have significant unexpected costs for maintenance and repair. For both of these reasons, if you decide to invest in rental real estate, that investment should be balanced with more liquid investments such as stocks and bonds.

Chapter 8: Portfolio Building Blocks – Annuities

Annuities are always great for the people who sell them. Sometimes they are also good for the people who buy them.

An annuity is a contract with an insurance company to receive a stream of payments in the future. There are two basic kinds of annuities: **fixed annuities** and **variable annuities**.

A **fixed annuity** can be thought of as the reverse of a regular life insurance policy. With a regular life insurance policy you are making a bet (even though you probably don't want to win it) that you will die and get a payoff. Depending on the type of policy, the insurance company is either betting that the insured will live and they won't have to pay (term insurance) or that you will live long enough that they can make more from investing the money than they have to pay out in claims (whole life). With fixed annuities, the bet is exactly the opposite. The buyer gives the insurance company a fixed amount of money, either in a single payment or over a period of time. The insurance company promises to pay a monthly amount for the rest of the insured person's life, either starting immediately or starting at a specified time in the future. If the buyer lives a short time after beginning to receive payments, it was a good deal for the insurance company; if the buyer lives a long time it was a good deal for the buyer. Insurance companies use statistical techniques to forecast the profitability of their annuity portfolios over the long run. Some annuities have what is called a "period certain." This means that the payments must be made for a certain period of time such as ten years or fifteen years, even if the annuitant dies during that period. If the annuitant dies, the payments are made to the beneficiary.

Fixed annuities are long-term investment vehicles usually designed for retirement purposes. Guarantees are based on the claims paying ability of the issuing company. Gains from tax deferred investments are taxable as ordinary income as withdrawn, and, if the annuity was purchased with tax-deferred assets (such as IRA assets) withdrawals before age 59 1/2 are subject to a 10% IRS penalty. In addition many annuities have significant surrender charges if withdrawals above a specified schedule are taken in the early years the annuity is purchased. If you are purchasing an annuity be very careful to fully understand the surrender charges and how much, if anything, you are allowed to withdraw before the surrender charges apply.

A very common type of fixed annuity is the Single Premium Immediate Annuity (SPIA). With this product the buyer makes one large payment and begins receiving payments the very next month.

A **variable annuity** can be thought of as an insurance policy with a package of investment options inside it. The investment options are kept in what are called "separate accounts" meaning that they are separate from the insurance part of the annuity. The value of the annuity goes up and down with the markets and the buyer usually has some choice about what investments will be in the separate accounts and how aggressive the investments will be. The annuity owner can usually change the annuity's investment allocations at reasonable intervals. Moving investments from one option to another inside the annuity does not create a tax event.

Annuities can also be **qualified** or **non-qualified**, depending on whether the money used to buy the annuity has already been taxed. An example of a qualified annuity would be one that was bought with funds in a traditional IRA. A qualified annuity works a lot like a traditional IRA in that the money is not taxed as long as it stays in the annuity and when you start getting distributions they are taxed as ordinary income. A non-qualified annuity works a lot like a Roth IRA in that the gain is not taxed while it stays in the annuity and when you start taking distributions the part allocated to "return of principal" is not taxable and the amount allocated to "gain" is taxable as ordinary income .

Annuities may be one of the most overused investments because they pay high commissions and have nice residual payments to the seller. Compliance departments at brokerage firms monitor carefully to be sure that advisors are not selling annuities inappropriately. That said, there are some situations where annuities are particularly appropriate.

Fixed annuities can be excellent if an investor is old enough (usually over 70) for the annuity to have a good rate of return and who has enough resources to meet his or her financial goal but who could be severely harmed by a market downturn. By moving part of the assets into a fixed annuity the investor can transfer part of the risk to the insurance company selling the annuity. The insurance company guarantees the contracted payments regardless of what happens in the stock market.

Variable annuities have a tax advantage. The gains in the separate account, regardless of whether they are income or capital gains, are not taxed as long as they remain in the annuity. For an investor who has taken advantage of all the tax deferred investments they can and still wants to put away more for retirement, a variable annuity provides a way to take advantage of additional tax deferral. Variable annuities can also be useful for very high income investors who want to be able to reallocate the investments in their portfolios without creating taxable income.

Variable annuities are long-term investment vehicles usually designed for retirement purposes. Guarantees are based on the claims paying ability of the issuing company. They have both an insurance and investment component and are sold only by prospectus. Gains from tax deferred investments are taxable as ordinary income as withdrawn, and, if the annuity was purchased with tax-deferred assets (such as IRA assets) withdrawals before age 59 1/2 are subject to a 10% IRS penalty. In addition many annuities have significant surrender charges if withdrawals above a specified schedule are taken in the early years the annuity is purchased. If you are purchasing an annuity be very careful to fully understand the surrender charges and how much, if anything, you are allowed to withdraw before the surrender charges apply. Since the securities in the "separate account" are market based securities, their value fluctuates. The value of an investor's unit when it is redeemed could be more or less than the original investment.

Chapter 9: Portfolio Building Blocks - Taxable and Tax Deferred Accounts

Investment accounts can be affected by a variety of tax rules, and most portfolios will include more than one type of account. It is important to understand the tax treatment of the various kinds of accounts so that investments can be distributed among the accounts to create optimum overall tax advantage. *In most cases, it is in the investor's interest to take advantage of tax deferred accounts for money that is intended for retirement or college funding.*

Taxable Accounts

A taxable account is a standard account at a brokerage that has no special tax status. All income earned by the account is taxed in the year it is earned as either ordinary income or capital gains. Gains in the value of securities in a portfolio are not taxed until they are "realized," that is, until the security is sold and the investor makes a profit.

Tax Deferred Retirement Accounts

The rules discussed in this section are what are in force as this book is being written. Since congress frequently changes the rules, it is advisable to check the current rules with a tax advisor before investing. The various types of accounts have contribution limits and some have income limitations.

Individual Accounts

Traditional Individual Retirement Accounts (IRA)

In a Traditional IRA an investor who qualifies can invest up to $5000 a year ($6000 if over 50 years of age) of "pre-tax" money. This means that the amount put into an IRA is deducted *before* the investor's income tax is computed. In addition, there is no tax on gains in the IRA as long as the assets remain in the account. Since the money in the account has never been taxed, it is taxed as ordinary income when it is withdrawn. Money can be withdrawn from a Traditional IRA when the investor reaches age 59

½ without any penalty. If it is withdrawn before that time, there is a 10% penalty in addition to having ordinary income tax. When the investor reaches age 70 ½ he or she is required to begin taking distributions of at least a minimum amount calculated by the IRS.

Consult a tax advisor about the qualification rules because they can be a bit complex. But, in general, if you are not in a company retirement plan you can invest up to the limit as long as what you invest is not more than your income.

Roth IRA

A Roth IRA is similar to a Traditional IRA except that the money is invested "after tax." There is still no tax on the gain while it stays in the account and withdrawals can be taken after age 59 ½ without penalty. For withdrawals considered qualified, the principal is not taxable because it has already been taxed, but the gain is taxable. Limitations and restrictions may apply. There is no requirement for minimum withdrawals at age 70 ½.

Employer Based Accounts

There are also retirement accounts that are managed by employers. There are a lot of limits and restrictions on these plans that are outside the scope of this book, but employees in organizations that offer them can easily obtain the documents that apply. The rules and limits are constantly changing, so it is important for business owners to consult a good financial advisor to help understand all the implications of setting up a plan. Here are some of the most common employer plan types:

401(k) and 403(b)

These two types of accounts are essentially the same. 401(k)'s are used in for-profit organizations and 403(b)'s are used in not-for-profit organizations. They allow an employee to set aside "pre-tax" money for a retirement account. This means that the money put into the account is deducted from the employee's income before the tax is calculated. In some cases employers match some or all of the employee's contribution to the retirement account. If an employer offers a match, it is almost always advisable for the employee to participate in the program, at least up to the point of the employer match, in order to take advantage of the employer contribution.

401(k)'s may also have a Roth option which allows the employee to contribute after-tax money instead of pre-tax money. This option has some tax benefits when withdrawals are made. There is another variation of the 401(k) called the Safe Harbor 401(k) that is designed to benefit the owners of small businesses.

SEP IRA's

A SEP IRA (Simplified Employee Pension) is a retirement plan in which *all* of the contributions are made by the employer. The contributions are tax deductible for the employer and grow tax deferred like and IRA. All contributions are immediately vested, meaning that the money in the account is owned by the employee.

Simple IRA's

A SIMPLE IRA (Savings Incentive Match Plan for Employees) is a combination plan that allows employees to contribute pre-tax money for retirement. Unlike a 401(k), employer contributions are required, not optional. The employer does have the option of either matching participating employees contributions up to a cap or making a contribution for all eligible employees whether they contribute or not.

457

This is a program specifically designed for government agencies and tax-exempt organizations, except for churches or church-controlled organizations. Employees may contribute pre-tax money which grows tax deferred. An important feature of 457's is that employees may contribute even if they are in another retirement plan and have a high income.

Early Retirement

Suppose you are younger than 59 ½ and want to retire early. There is a provision in the law for people who have a tax deferred retirement account to retire before 59 ½. This is called a 72(t) retirement after the section of the IRS code.   If you want to retire early, the IRS has a formula that calculates the minimum amount you must take each month as your distribution.   In addition, you must agree to continue the minimum payments for at least 5 years.   If you stop sooner there is a tax penalty. Once the five years is up, you have the option of discontinuing the payments or changing the amount

Taxed Deferred Education Funding
529 Accounts

Investments in 529 accounts are made with after-tax money, i.e. there is no tax deduction for the contribution.   However, the gains are not taxable while they remain in the account and withdrawals are not subject to federal tax if they are spent on qualified higher education expenses.   State tax treatment varies.   A 529 account has an owner and a beneficiary.   The beneficiary is the child whose education will be funded.   The beneficiary can be changed at any time as long as the new beneficiary is a sibling of the current beneficiary, so families can have one account to take care of all their children.

Prior to investing in a 529 plan you should investigate whether the home state of either the owner of the beneficiary of the plan offers special tax benefits that are only available to that state's qualified   tuition program.   Consult your tax advisor before investing in a 529 plan so you can fully understand the implications for your state.

An interesting thing to keep in mind is that, if the owner of the 529 is a parent, the account must be declared as an "asset" when financial aid eligibility is calculated.   However, if the account were owned by anyone else, such as a grandparent, aunt, or uncle, the account does not have to be declared.   Also, once an account is established anyone can contribute to it.

Chapter 10: Rules for Helping to Increase the Rate of Return

There is no guarantee that any approach to investing, including this one, will achieve positive results. Strategies that have worked in the past may not work the same way in the future. Many advisors may disagree with some of the techniques outlined here. Nevertheless, *it is important to have a strategy rather than invest randomly and it is advisable to review your strategy with an advisor whom you trust.* If you are doing your own investing you can pay for an hour or two of an advisor's time to get a second set of eyes on your plan.

Here are some basic guidelines to follow as you develop your portfolio:

Follow the Principles for Managing Risk

One of the most important ways to help increase your rate of return is to reduce the likelihood of a substantial negative impact. Managing risk is critically important in achieving your life goals.

Focus on Current Yield

Current yield is the income your portfolio receives for interest, dividends, limited partnership payments, and similar sources. An important thing to remember is that **income** is **not** the same as **distributions**. In many investments distributions can include return of capital. *Caution: Some investors confuse the two and spend distributions thinking they are income, thereby inadvertently depreciating their assets.*

Minimize the Use of Mutual Funds

Investing in mutual funds involves risk including possible loss of principal. In addition, there are seven different kinds of costs associated with mutual funds:

1. **Sales charges** – These are the charges you pay to buy into the fund originally. They can be paid all up-front or with an annual fee.

Depending on the size of your purchase and the fund, up-front charges can range from 0 to 5.75%. If the sales charges are paid on an annual basis, it usually runs in the range of 0.7% to 0.8% additional annual charge on top of the management fee.

2. **Management Fees** - Actively managed funds charge an annual fee that may range for 0.25% to 2% depending on the complexity of the fund. This pays the people who manage the fund.

3. **12(b)1 Fee** – This is a sales and support fee. It is usually shared with the selling broker to pay for ongoing support of the investment and it is in addition to the management fee.

4. **Transaction Charges** – These are brokerage commissions, usually paid to an affiliate of the company that manages the fund.

5. **Cash Drag** –If the fund manager leaves a significant portion of the fund in cash, that portion is earning very little return. Cash drag is the opportunity cost (the lack of interest, dividends, or capital gains) associated with the portion of the fund that is not invested at any given time.

6. **Phantom Income** – When a fund manager generates interest or dividends or creates capital gains by selling assets that have increased in value, taxable income is created. If the income is reinvested rather than being distributed, the shareholder must find other sources of cash to pay the taxes.

7. **End of Day Trading** – Unlike stocks and bonds, if you decide to sell shares in a fund during the day, you don't sell it at the price at that particular time. The net asset value (NAV) is calculated at the end of the trading day and that is the price you receive. On a day when the market is dropping significantly your morning sell order cannot be executed until after the market closes.

An important note about mutual fund fees: while critics of funds put a lot of focus on the sales charge, *over the long term the annual fees can have much greater impact.* Let's look at a hypothetical example of a 1% combined gross annual expense on a $250,000 portfolio compounded for 30 years. This means that, if the gross return on a fund is 7%, the investor will receive 6% after the fee. At 7% the value after 30 years would be $2,172,551; at an after fee 6% the value would be $1, 582,967. That would mean it cost the investor $589,584 for the privilege of using the fund for 30 years. To justify that cost, the investor would have to believe that he or she could not have achieved a return better than 6% without the help of a fund manager.

The Chartered Financial Analyst training materials put it very succinctly:

> "Mutual funds perform, on average, similar to the market before considering fees and expenses and perform worse than the market, on average, once fees and expenses are considered."[9]

In spite of this fact, many financial advisors build the core of their practice on selling mutual funds. Why is this? Likely for one or more of three reasons:

- It is less work
- Their share of the 12b1 fees gives them regular income
- They don't feel competent to pick stocks and bonds themselves

Any financial advisor worth his or her salt should be competent to build a properly diversified portfolio of large cap developed world stocks and investment grade bonds. **There is no need to pay fund fees for these classes of investment.**

There some situations where the use of mutual funds might be appropriate despite the costs. For example:

1. The size of the client's portfolio is not sufficient to allow for adequate diversification. In this case, the client can achieve instant diversification by using one or more mutual funds.
2. There is a good strategic reason to include less common classes of investment in the portfolio (e.g. dividend-paying emerging market companies or diversified international bonds). The generalist financial advisor may not have access to enough information to make judgments about investments like these, and therefore may want to engage a specialist in the form of a fund manager.

---

[9] Cleary, W. Sean, CFA, Howard Atkinson, CFA, and Pamela Peterson Drake, CFA "Market Efficiency" in *Equity and Fixed Income, CFA Program Curriculum Volume 5*, CFA Institute, 2011

Include a Few Carefully Selected Aggressive Investments

The mathematical basis for this rule is easy to understand. Example: a total portfolio is $100,000. 98% of the portfolio has a 7% return and 2% of the portfolio is put into an investment that could have a 20% return or could be lost entirely. What would be the results if the value were lost and if the high return were achieved? If the aggressive investment lost all value, the 7% return on the $98,000 would mean a 6.86% return on the whole $100,000, a downside of 0.14%. But if the aggressive investment achieved the 20% return, the return on the whole $100,000 would be 7.26%, an upside of 0.26%. So the upside is almost twice the downside. Of course, this is an oversimplified hypothetical example to illustrate the point. But some carefully selected aggressive investments can really help the overall return, *as long as the portfolio results will still be acceptable if the aggressive investments don't work out.*

Use Market Overreactions as Opportunities

One of Warren Buffet's most quoted sayings is, "Be fearful when everyone else is greedy and greedy when everyone else is fearful." When the market wildly overreacts like it did in 2008-2009, it makes sense to take advantage of that potential opportunity. In that case, it definitely made sense to shift the asset allocation temporarily to take advantage of the expected market recovery. For example, if a portfolio were 60% stocks and 40% bonds, if could make sense to shift the ratio to 80%/20%. Then, as the gains are accrued, the portfolio can be gradually returned to its original allocations. This is an example of the tactical reallocation we discussed earlier. Tactical allocation may involve more frequent buying and selling of assets and, therefore, depending on what type of account you have, may mean higher transaction costs. Also, when the assets that are bought and sold are not in a tax-deferred account, there could be tax consequences.

One such opportunity occurred in 2010 when a respected analyst incorrectly predicted that there would be a high number of municipal bond defaults. Prices on municipal bonds dropped and yields jumped. This was an opportunity to increase the current yield on a portfolio by picking up some high yield investment grade muni bonds. The analyst's prediction turned out to be wrong and those investors who took advantage of the opportunity either locked in a higher yield or could re-allocate the increase in value back to other assets and take a profit. (Remember, with bonds, when prices go down yields go up and *vice versa*.)

Be Tax-Efficient

The simplest way to help reduce the tax impact on a portfolio is to look at the portfolio as a whole and put the investments that generate current income, such as taxable bonds and high dividend stocks, REITs, and Limited Partnerships, in tax deferred accounts. The taxable accounts can be used for assets designed primarily to generate long term capital gains. That way the investor has control over when a tax event occurs. Also, tax free muni bonds should be in taxable accounts – putting them in tax deferred accounts wastes the tax benefit.

Chapter 11: Some Approaches to Designing your Portfolio

"A good portfolio is more than a long list of good stocks and bonds. It is a balanced whole, providing the investor with protections and opportunities with respect to a wide range of contingencies." **Harry Markowitz**

The Factors that Determine your Portfolio

- Your goals and your analysis of the amount of money needed for the goals and the amount of time required to accumulate the money.
- Your ability to absorb losses in market downturns and still achieve the goals. This means the closer you get to the goal the more conservative you need to be
- Your ability to maintain confidence during market fluctuations.
- Your age and stage of life.

How the Big Kids Do It

As a learning exercise, let's take a look at how a couple of the folks who manage billion dollar portfolios structure their investments. Then we can take extract a few lessons for those of us who manage more ordinary amounts of assets. But remember, no strategy assures success or guarantees against loss.

Harvard Management Company

The Harvard Management Company manages the multi-billion dollar Harvard endowment. They make their strategy public on the web at www.hmc.harvard.edu . Here is their 2012 portfolio allocation.

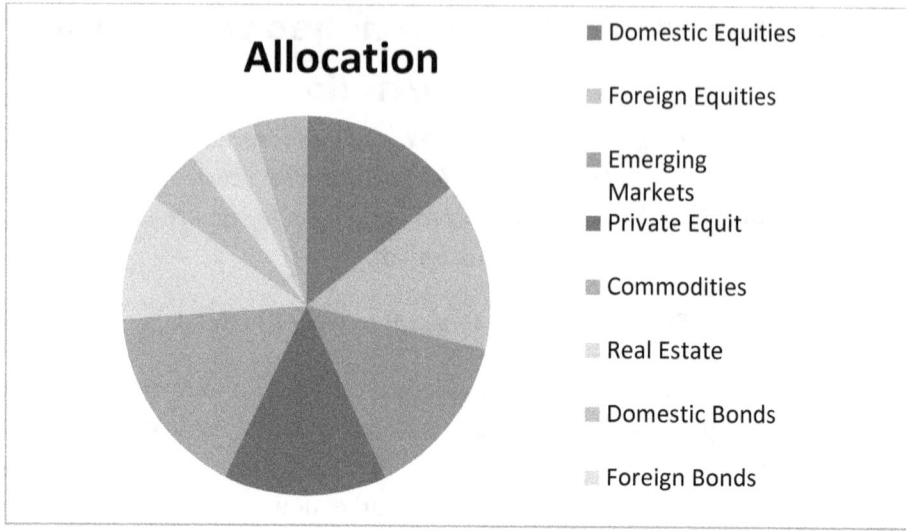

Allocation

- Domestic Equities
- Foreign Equities
- Emerging Markets
- Private Equit
- Commodities
- Real Estate
- Domestic Bonds
- Foreign Bonds

Notice that their allocation includes large proportions of alternative investments. To manage a portfolio of this complexity requires a large staff that can stay on top of these more esoteric investments. What is the lesson we can learn? To help increase return it may be advisable to look beyond just stocks and bonds. But without a large staff it would be advisable to use funds for these investments and to keep them down to a small percentage of the portfolio.

Some important disclosures for this kind of allocation:

Of course, like any other kind of stock investing there is risk including possible loss of principal.

International and emerging market investing involves special risks such as currency fluctuation and political instability, so it may not be appropriate for all investors.

Private equity is considered an "Alternative Investment." Alternative investments may not be suitable for all investors and, if used, should be considered as part of the higher risk portion of an investor's portfolio. The strategies used in the management of alternative investments (e.g. leverage) can accelerate the velocity of potential losses.

The fast price swings in commodities and currencies will result in significant volatility in an investor's holdings.

Investing in Real Estate Investment Trusts (REITs), especially REITs not publicly traded on an exchange, involves special risks such as potential illiquidity and may not be suitable for all investors. There is no assurance that the manager's stated objectives will be attained.

And, of course, bonds are subject to market and interest rate risks if sold prior to maturity and will decline in value as interest rates rise.

High yield/junk bonds (graded BB or below) are not investment grade securities and are subject to higher credit, interest rate and liquidity risks than those graded BBB and above. The generally should be used as part of a diversified portfolio for sophisticated investors.

Treasury Inflation Protected Securities (TIPS) help eliminate inflation risk for your portfolio as the principal is adjusted semiannually based on the Consumer Price Index while providing a real rate of return guaranteed by the US Government.

No strategy assures success or guarantees protection against loss.

JP Morgan Asset Management

In a booklet they provide as a reference for financial advisors, JP Morgan Asset Management compares two portfolios. One they call the "Traditional Portfolio" and the other "More Diversified Portfolio." Their analysis generally shows that the more diversified portfolio has a higher return and a lower standard deviation. (They still use standard deviation as a measure of risk, perhaps because they haven't read this book – just kidding.) Here are the two portfolios:[10]

---

[10] JP Morgan Asset Management, *Guide to the Markets, 4Q 2011*, October 2011 p 57

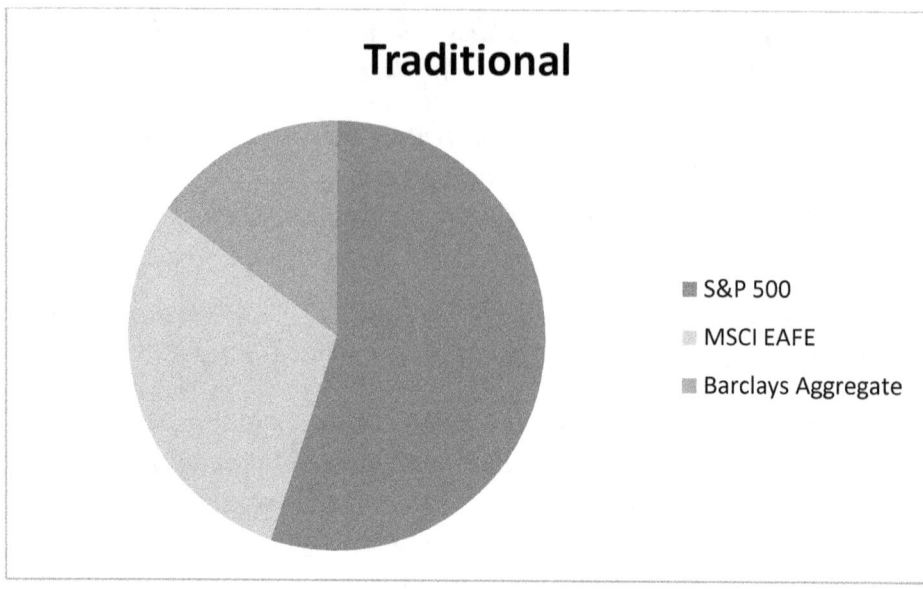

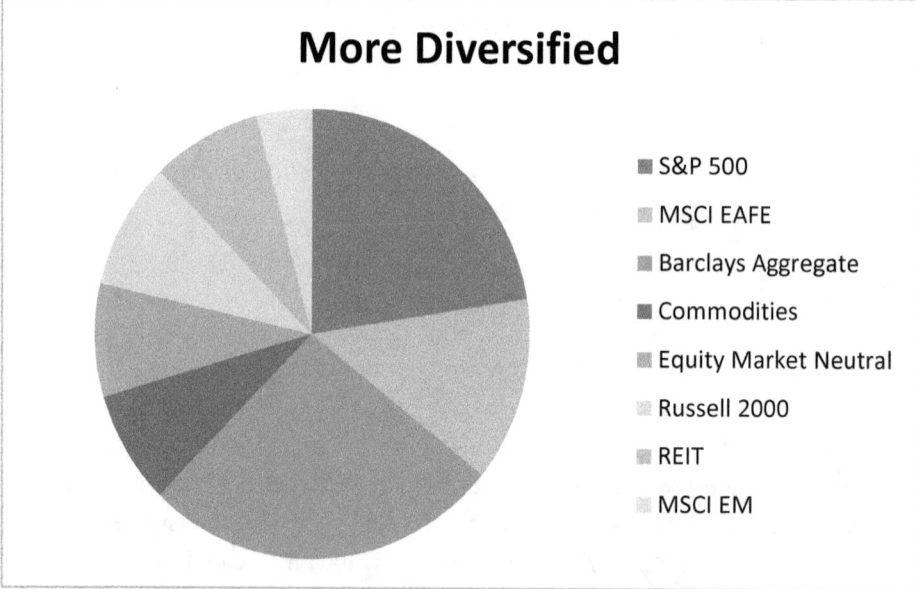

Let's go through what some of those mean. MSCI EAFE and EM are indexes of large cap foreign stocks and emerging market stocks respectively; Barclays Aggregate is an index of bonds; and the Russell 2000 is an index that incorporates mid-cap stocks. The purpose of adding the additional categories of investment is to attempt to add investments that have a lower correlation to the major categories of domestic stocks, foreign stocks, and bonds. The data say that this strategy, if done correctly, can improve the portfolio's overall return. Remember, indexes are unmanaged and investors are not able to invest directly into any index.

Some important disclosures to this kind of allocation:

Again, like any other kind of stock investing there is risk including possible loss of principal.

International and emerging market investing involves special risks such as currency fluctuation and political instability, so it may not be appropriate for all investors.

Stocks of mid-cap companies are subject to higher volatility than those of large cap companies

Bonds are subject to market and interest rate risk if sold prior to maturity and bond values will decline as interest rates rise.

The fast price swings in commodities and currencies will result in significant volatility in a portfolio.

"Equity Market Neutral" is a form of alternative investment. As always, alternative investments may not be suitable for all investors and, and if used, should be considered as part of the higher risk portion of a portfolio as the strategies used in the management of alternative investments can accelerate the velocity of losses.

Some Real Estate Investment Trusts are not publicly traded on an exchange. This means that if you want to sell your interest you have to find a buyer willing to purchase it. Investing in these REIT's involves special risks including possible illiquidity and therefore may not be appropriate for all investors. There is no assurance that the objectives of these programs will be achieved.

No strategy assures success or protects against loss.

Include Some Fixed Income

In my practice I have encountered investors in their 50's, 60's and even 70's whose portfolios consisted entirely of equities. They had no fixed income- no bonds. That made them extremely vulnerable to downturns in the market like what happened in 2008.

We will get into what size this portion should be when we discuss stress testing your portfolio.

The 80/20 approach

In this approach a minimum of 80% of your portfolio will consist of large and mid-cap, dividend paying equities and investment grade bonds. The equities portion should consist primarily of large cap US or multinational company stocks with small portions of REIT's and Limited Partnerships. The investment grade bonds should mostly be rated A- or higher with the option of a small portion of BBB's.

Once the 80% or more is allocated, you can use the remainder to try to increase the return (add more aggressive investments), protect the principal (add more conservative investments), or both. For the more aggressive investment you might use small cap or emerging market stocks. In these cases it is appropriate to use mutual funds or exchange traded funds (EFT's), since investments like emerging market stocks are harder to manage. You might also consider a few high yield bonds (rated BB+ or lower). For the more conservative investments you might use cash or inflation protected US treasuries. *No more than 10% at the very most should be in aggressive investments.*

How do you decide what the percentages of equities (stocks, REIT's, LP's) and fixed income (bonds, CD's) should be? Here's one way to approach it. As a starting point set the percentage of fixed income at your age minus 20, for example, if you are 50 years old you would have 70% equities and 30% fixed income. Then think about how you would deal with substantial negative variance in the value of your portfolio. For example, if the value dropped 10% or even 20%, would you be able to maintain confidence in a long term investment plan or would you be strongly tempted to sell? If this kind of variance would be extremely stressful for you, than adjust the fixed income allocation upward by 5% and think it through again. Remember, as you add fixed income you increase potential downside protection but you also sacrifice upside potential. And don't forget about inflation.

Required disclosures for the 80/20 approach: (sorry for the repetition, but FINRA requires it for your protection)

Stock investing involves risk including possible loss of principal;

Stocks of mid-cap companies are subject to higher volatility that those of large cap companies.

Bonds are subject to market and interest rate risk if sold prior to maturity and their prices will decline as interest rate rise.

High yield or junk bonds (those rated BB or lower) are not considered investment grade securities and are subject to higher market and credit risk than those rated BBB or higher. They generally should be part of a diversified portfolio for sophisticated investors.

Treasury Inflation Protected Securities (TIPS) help eliminate inflation risk to your portfolio as the principal is adjusted semiannually for inflation based on the Consumer Price Index while providing a real rate of return guaranteed by the U.S. government.

International investing involves special risks such as currency fluctuation and political instability and may not be suitable for all investors.

Investing in Real Estate Investment Trusts involves special risks such as potential illiquidity and may not be suitable for all investors. There is no assurance that the objectives of a program will be attained.

Limited partnerships are subject to special risks such as potential illiquidity and may not be suitable for all investors.

Investing in mutual funds involves risk including possible loss of principal.

An investment in Exchange Traded Funds (ETF), structured as a mutual fund or unit investment trust, involves the risk of losing money and should be considered as part of an overall program, not a complete investment program. An investment in ETFs involves additional risks such as lack of diversification, price volatility, competitive industry pressure, international political and economic developments, possible trading halts, and index tracking errors.

No strategy assures either success or protection against loss.

Diversifying the Equities

The equities portion of the portfolio should consist of 20-30 different equities with at least some representation from all of the economic sectors. If the size of the portfolio does not reasonably allow for that many stocks, a fund might be appropriate.

One way to start your selection is to find the stock in each market sector that pays the highest dividend. Then analyze each company's financial statements to be sure the dividend is sustainable. Then add stocks with good dividends that are rated "buy" by one of the analyst services. Be sure you have not seriously over-weighted any one economic sector without having a good reason to do so. Remember dividends are not guaranteed and companies may decrease or eliminate dividends at any time.

Diversifying the Bonds

The bonds should be diversified by three criteria: issuer, sector, and maturity. No issuer should represent more than 5% of the entire portfolio. *If the portfolio is not large enough for there to be 10 different issuers, you should consider using a bond unit investment trust or bond mutual fund.* No more than a third of the bonds should have issuers in any one industry such as banks or utilities. The largest portion of the bonds should be concentrated in mid-term maturities, this is from 5 to 15 years. However, if current income is the primary goal of the portfolio and your age is such that you would not expect to live more than 20 more years, going for higher yields by having longer terms may be appropriate. This is because the primary risk associated with longer terms is greater reduction in market value if interest rates rise. If the bonds are not expected to be sold during the holder's lifetime, this risk becomes less important.

Stress Testing Your Draft Portfolio

Once you have a list of investments, enter them into a spreadsheet so you can run some tests. Divide the equities into economic sectors and divide the bonds into groups by 5 year maturities (5-10 years, 11-15 years, etc.). Now take each sector of the economy and see what happens to the total portfolio value if every equity in that sector loses 25%. Are there any results that you would be unwilling to tolerate? If so, reduce the amount allocated to those sectors and increase the amount allocated to some other sectors. The stress test for the bonds involves the impact of interest rates. Assume the market value of the 5-10 year bonds drops by 5%, the 11-15 year bonds by 10%, and everything longer than 15 years by 15%. Is that a risk you can tolerate? If not, replace some of the longer maturities with shorter maturities.

After a few iterations you should be able to settle on your portfolio allocations. Then see if your draft portfolio will be able to address your goals if the long term return is 4% for the fixed income portion and 8% for the equity portion. If the answer is no, then you are in a conflict between your goal and your risk tolerance. You will have to decide whether to scale back the goals or learn to live with more stress than you would prefer. If your draft portfolio exceeds the amount required to achieve the goals, then change the portfolio to more conservative allocations. Remember our principle, **as much risk as is required to address your goal and no more.**

You can now set the model allocations for your portfolio. Set the percentages of equity and fixed income, the sector allocations of the equities, and the maturity allocations of the fixed income.

Adjusting the Allocation

As the market works its wonders, the values in your portfolio will inevitably diverge from the model. You will need to reallocate periodically to bring the values back into line. In the absence of dramatic shifts in the market twice a year should be often enough to reallocate. But if any segment increases in value by more than 20%, it would be a good idea to take some profits and spend them by adding to the segments that have declined. If you follow this discipline you will generally be buying low and selling high. That is, after all, what we all want to do. However, rebalancing does not assure either success or protection against loss.

Chapter 12: Conventional Investment Theory and Why It's Wrong

"The only way they look at risk is in the rearview mirror."

Conventional investing strategies from the 1960's through the market collapse of 2008 have been based on the three pillars of **The Efficient Market Hypothesis, the Capital Asset Pricing Model, and Modern Portfolio Theory**. Among them they won multiple Nobel prizes in economics for their discoverers. But as a basis for practical investing they have been an abysmal failure.

The Efficient Market Hypothesis

The Efficient Market Hypothesis (EMH) was developed in the 1960's by Eugene Fama of the University of Chicago. This theory holds that the market as a whole is always right and that whatever price the market assigns to a particular security incorporates all of the information available at the time. When new information is discovered, the market absorbs it quickly and incorporates it into a new price. EMH further holds that any variations in price that are not based on new fundamental information must be random.

Many analysts believe that EMH contributed significantly to the severity of the 2008-2009 financial crisis. The problem was this: EMH said that the market could not continue to deteriorate once the decline was not supported by fundamental information. For example, when there were some companies with market capitalization (the total value of all their outstanding stock) lower than their intrinsic value (the amount for which the company's assets could be sold), the market would correct that mispricing very quickly. Because, if it didn't, that would mean the market was acting irrationally. Oops! The stock stayed mispriced for months.

In an excellent critique of EMH Benoit Mandelbrot[11] cites four reasons why EMH fails.

- First, investors are not always rational. For example, panic selling is an emotionally driven, not a rationally driven behavior.

- Second, investors are not all alike, and do not have the same goals, methods, or time horizons. When researchers have modeled systems that do not assume all investors are alike the results have been "a chaotic 'non-linear' system."[12] Stock prices in the last quarter of 2008 and the first quarter of 2009 were chaotic.

- Third, stock prices do not always change continuously in small increments. Sometimes they take large jumps, even in the absence of significant information. The "flash crash" of 2010 was only one example.

- Fourth, price changes are not random and do not follow the standard bell curve.

Without getting too deeply into the math of it, if the equations of EMH were correct, a bubble (certain classes of assets being priced irrationally high) should occur about once every 44 years. But in reality there have been 30 in the last 85 years – more often than one year out of three![13]

As the crisis of 2008 began to unfold, one of the problems was that many professional investors were EMH adherents and believed that the disorder had to be short-lived. How wrong they were!

One of the most spectacular failures of EMH was the collapse of Long Term Capital Management (LTCM) in the 1990's. The fund was founded on the EMH doctrine that, if the prices of similar securities diverge, the market will cause them to converge quickly. When the convergence failed to happen as predicted, the fund lost billions and had to be bailed out.

---

[11] Mandelbrot, Benoit and Richard Hudson, *The (Mis)behavior of Markets*, Basic Books, New York, 2004

[12] Ibid. 85

[13] Montier, James *The Little Book of Behavioral Investing*, John Wiley & Sons, Hoboken, 2010 p130

LTCM had been founded by two Nobel Prize winners, Robert Merton and Myron Scholes. After the crash they disclaimed responsibility saying that the collapse was caused by a "ten sigma event," meaning ten standard deviations below the average in probability. Nassim Nicholas Taleb, the author of *Black Swan*, makes an interesting critique of this claim:

> "Someone saying this is a ten sigma either (a) knows what he is talking about with near perfection ...knows his probabilities, and it is an event that happens once every several times in the history of the universe; or (b) does not know what he is talking about (with a high degree of certainty) and it is an event that has a higher probability than once every several times in the history of the universe. I will let the reader pick from these two mutually exclusive interpretations which is more plausible."[14]

The Capital Asset Pricing Model

The Capital Asset Pricing Model (CAPM), also developed in the 1960's, claims to be a method of assessing the value of adding any particular investment to a portfolio. CAPM is based on a series of assumptions, all of which have been proven to be incorrect. Here are those flawed assumptions:[15]

1. **There are no transaction costs.** Clearly this is not the case for individual investors.
2. **Investors can take either buy or sell short any amount of any stock or bond without affecting the market.** We know that short selling funds take large positions with the explicit intention of affecting the market. To cite just one example, in 1991 the head of bond trading at Salomon Brothers was forced to resign because the Federal Government feared Salomon Brothers was buying and

---

[14] Taleb, Nassim Nicholas, *Fooled by Randomness:The Hidden Role of Chance in Life and in the Markets*, Random House, New York, 2005 p242

[15] Montier, James, *Behavioral Finance:Insights into Irrational Minds and Markets*, John Wiley, West Sussex, 2002 p86

selling large blocks in order to affect the price of Treasury bonds.

3. **There are no taxes**. We all know how untrue this is.

4. **All investors are risk averse**. Many investors have a large appetite for risk and intentionally take very risky positions in the hope of a large reward. Many funds exist for the expressed purpose of buying other people's risks; that's where the name "Hedge Fund" comes from.

5. **Investors all share a common time horizon**. In fact, investors vary greatly in their time horizons; some invest for minutes and others for decades.

6. **All investors define risk in terms of historical volatility** using metrics like mean and standard deviation. There is no data to support this assumption. It is likely that investors use a wide variety of ways, consciously or unconsciously, of defining risk for their investment purposes.

7. **Investors can lend and borrow continuously at the "risk free" rate** (the rate paid by U.S. government securities). In fact, investors borrow from their brokerages at much higher rates to buy securities "on Margin". The value of the loans must stay below a given percentage of the value of the securities. So when prices fall, the margin investor gets a "margin call". This means he has to either deposit more cash or sell the securities to bring the percentage back in line. Margin calls can have enormous impact on the market and can create waves of selling.

From these CAPM assumptions the theory develops something called "The Efficient Frontier", a line on a graph that shows the investments with the highest reward/risk ratio. That means an investment on that line will have the highest return for a given level of risk or the lowest risk for a given level of return.

The CAPM assumptions offer a great deal of convenience for someone who wants to apply sophisticated statistical techniques to financial analysis. The assumptions substantially simplify the mathematics. There is one problem, however. The data doesn't support them. The theory says a one day swing in the Dow of more than 7% should happen about once every 300,000 years. In fact it happened 48 times in just the 20th century.[16]

Both EMH and CAPM require that price changes not based on changes in fundamental information must be random, independent variables. In fact the data show that price changes are neither random nor independent. "Large price changes tend to be followed by more large changes, positive or negative. Small changes tend to be followed by more small changes."[17] In other words, the market easily develops momentum that defies logic.

That leaves us with some interesting conclusions about CAPM:

1. Historical volatility (how much the stock price changes day-to-day) is not a valid measure for risk. The data just doesn't support it.
2. If historical volatility is not a valid metric, then there is no Efficient Frontier, because the whole concept of Efficient Frontier is based on historic volatility.
3. If there is no Efficient Frontier CAPM fails as method for choosing investments for a portfolio.

Modern Portfolio Theory

Modern Portfolio Theory (MPT) was developed by Professor Harry Markowitz at the Rand Corporation in the 1950's. It became the topic of his doctoral dissertation in 1955 and was further developed in a densely famous mathematical paper published in 1959. To some extent both EMH and CAPM were based on the work of Markowitz, work which won him the Nobel Memorial Prize in Economics.

The core error of his work is the complete confusion of **risk** with **uncertainty** and **uncertainty** with **volatility (variance)** as measured either

---

[16] Mandelbrot, Benoit and Richard Hudson, *The (Mis)Behavior of Markets*, Basic Books, New York, 2004 p 13
[17] Ibid p 248

by past volatility or the opinions about future volatility on the part of so-called experts. In fact, in the index of his book *Portfolio Selection*, the listing "Uncertainty" says "see risk."

Let's look at some basic definitions from the perspective of an individual investor, not an expert in higher mathematics. I think most investors would define "risk" as the probability of incurring a significant loss. "Variance" (volatility) is a measure of how much the price of a security varies from day-to-day, week-to-week, or month-to-month. Implicit in the assumptions of MPT is that reducing variance is the optimal way to minimize risk.

Markowitz admits in the very last paragraphs of his paper that one of his goals was to simplify by reducing the number of variables because "Simplicity of analysis means less work in developing inputs, less computing time in obtaining the outputs."[18] (Back then scholars had to pay for computer time and feed the computers stacks of punched cards and heaven help you if you dropped the stack on the way to the computer lab.) But he then immediately admits, "Simplicity, however, can be bought at too high a price." *Black Swan* author, Nassim Nicholas Taleb reports on the impact of this oversimplification: "An immediate result of Dr. Markowitz's theory was the near collapse of the financial system in 1998."[19]

As an alternative to historic volatility, Markowitz suggests the possibility of using the consensus opinions of experts, using the assumption that the opinions will vary on a bell curve with the truth in the middle. Again, his assumption fails the reality test. James Montier's research shows that, "When an analyst first makes a forecast for a company's earnings two years prior to the actual event, they are on average wrong by a staggering 94 percent. Even at a 12-month time horizon they are wrong by around 45%! To put it mildly, analysts don't have a clue about future earnings."[20]

---

[18] Markowitz, Harry M., *Portfolio Selection: Efficient Diversification of Investments*, Yale University Press, New Haven, 1959 (Second printing 1970) p303
[19] Taleb (2005) p241
[20] Montier (2010) p59

The relationship between volatility and risk

High volatility (high variance) can *contribute* to risk if the time horizon of the investment could cause the investor to need to sell at a point when the investment is in one of its low cycles. **This is exactly the reason why a good financial advisor will advise that the portfolio become more conservative as the investor comes closer to the time when the investment proceeds will be needed for the goal.** The shorter the time horizon, the higher the probability of being forced to sell in a down market.

- If an investment has a high probability of increasing in value over the long term and also has high volatility, it may not be particularly risky if the investor is twenty years away from the goal. But if the investor is two years from the goal, it could be very risky.
- Low volatility not only does not assure low risk, it doesn't even necessarily give a higher probability of low risk. In fact, there are cases where low volatility leads to more risk. Nassim Taleb cites an example in currency trading: "currencies that exhibit the largest historical stability are the most prone to crashes."[21] The assumption even defies common sense. If the price of a stock has not varied much in the last few years, does that, in and of itself, mean that there is a low probability that the stock will not lose value in the future?
- Studies have also shown that volatility tends to increase in the periods before and after market crashes. That means that a sudden change in the level of volatility could be an indicator that the market is entering a period of increased risk.[22] That does not mean that the volatility caused the risk, it more likely means that the increased perception of risk caused the volatility.

---

[21] Taleb, Nassim Nicholas, *Fooled by Randomness; The Hidden Role of Chance in Life and in the Markets*, Random House, New York, 2005
[22] Montier, (2002) p142

What should not be forgotten in investing is the confidence factor involved with volatility. In his book, *Asset Allocation*[23], Roger Gibson suggests thinking about volatility tolerance as separate from risk tolerance. No investment is worth the return if you can't sleep at night. So even though a relatively high volatility investment may be theoretically appropriate for a specific investing situation, it may create too much stress for some investors. Remember, investment strategy should be in service of life goals, and that includes sleeping at night.

Volatility and Compounding

One contribution of modern portfolio theory is that it clearly demonstrates that volatility negatively affects the compounding of returns.

Let's take a quick look at what compounding means. If you invest $100 at 10% interest, at the end of a year you get $10 and have $110. If you leave the interest in the account, in the second year you get 10% of $110 or $11; in the third year you get 10% of $121 or $12.10; and so on. If you investment time horizon is 30 years, compounding can make an enormous difference. In this same example, $10,000 at 10% simple interest for 30 years would give you $30,000 in interest plus your original $10,000 for a total of $40,000. If the 10% were compounded annually you would have $174,484! Big difference!

The math of how volatility reduces the effect of compounding gets a bit complicated, so we won't go into it here. But the effect of compounding is important, so even though volatility is not the same as risk, it is worth your while to make the effort to reduce the volatility of your portfolio.

---

[23] Gibson, Roger, Asset Allocation: Balancing Financial Risk, McGraw-Hill, New York, 2008

Chapter 13: Finding and Using a Financial Advisor

Deciding Whether You Need a Financial Advisor

Whether you do it yourself or you hire someone to do it, the same tasks need to be done in designing a portfolio to meet your goals. Let's look at what those tasks are and what skills are required to perform the tasks.

1. **Define your life goals so that the statement meets the S.M.A.R.T criteria.**
2. **Evaluate your current resources**
3. **Develop a plan to address the goals and test it for reasonableness and achievability.**
4. **Design the portfolio to implement the plan in a way that is tailored to help reduce unnecessary risk**
5. **Review the portfolio periodically to see if it is on track to address the goals.**
6. **Make adjustments as necessary.**

Defining the goals so they meet the S.M.A.R.T. (Specific, Measurable, Achievable, Relevant, Time-bound) criteria requires a certain amount of skill with language and logic. Do you have that? Would you be good at making clear statements?

The skills required to evaluate your current resources depend on how complicated they are. If they consist primarily of savings accounts, that is not too hard. On the other hand, you might have a range of investments that came from inheritances, employee stock option plans, old 401(k) or 403(b) plans, and some rollover IRA's. Some or all of them may not be suitable for your new portfolio. Do you know enough about the world of securities to evaluate them and can you do it objectively? How much you may have loved the uncle who left you the stock has nothing to do with whether it is good for your portfolio. Also, long participation in employee stock option plans can lead to large holdings of stock in your current or former employer which can, in turn, lead to a portfolio that is out of balance.

Developing a good plan requires a broad knowledge of the various classes of securities, especially their risk and return characteristics and their correlations to each other.

Minimizing risk requires understanding the various types of risk and their probabilities of occurring. Sometimes protecting against one risk (e.g. reinvestment risk) can leave you more vulnerable to anther risk (e.g. interest rate risk).

If you can do these tasks with a reasonable level of confidence, it is realistic to believe you can put together your own financial plan. If not, it might be good to get some professional help.

How to Find a Financial Advisor

The best way to start is to ask a few people you know and respect if they are using an advisor and if they are happy with that advisor. That should provide you with a list of prospects. Then set up a series of interviews and approach them from the attitude that you are an employer considering hiring an employee. Or, put another way, you are the CEO of your assets and you are looking to hire a CFO. I would recommend interviewing at least three so you can get a good sense of what they have in common and how they differ.

It's your money and it needs to be managed the way you want it managed. So the key thing in finding an advisor is finding someone who works the way you want to work. It is definitely not about you fitting into the way the advisor wants to work - there are plenty of advisors out there, so you have plenty of options. For example, if you agree with the ideas proposed in this book such as minimizing the use of mutual funds, you want an advisor who is willing to build portfolios of individual stocks and bonds. That can be time consuming and it deprives them of their 12(b)1 trails (the amount the mutual fund pays the advisor to service your account).

Never make a decision at the first meeting. Any important component of an advisor's skill set is the ability to sell. Many are very good at it. So even if you are very impressed, take a few days to let the emotional impact of the first meet subside, then make your decision.

How to Evaluate Prospective Financial Advisors

The three most important things about having a financial advisor are:

- Do you trust him or her to be do what is in your best interest, even if it is not the way for them to make the most money?
- Will he or she take the time to tailor your plan specifically to your goals and your situation, not plug you in to some standard program?
- Can you can communicate effectively? If you leave a session feeling unheard or not understanding what the advisor said – keep looking.

FINRA and Types of Registration

The Financial Industry Regualtory Authority (FINRA) is an independent regulating agency that oversees the operations of the investment industry in the United States. All registered representatives and the firms they work for must be registered with FINRA and abide by FINRA regulations. In order to become registered the representative must pass an examination and a background check. FINRA also keeps public records of complaints against representatives and how those complaints were resolved. Before taking on an advisor you should go to www.finra.org and see if any complaints have been filed against that advisor.

FINRA offers a range of registrations to financial advisors. Each involves passing a test, and some tests are much more difficult than others. You want an advisor whose decisions about what investments to put in your portfolio are not limited by the registrations he or she holds. For example, an advisor's registration may allow them to sell mutual funds, but not individual stocks and bonds. The broadest registration is the Series 7 which permits selling many types of securities. If annuities are potentially part of your plan, the advisor must also be licensed to sell life insurance in your state.

How Financial Advisors Get Paid

There are variations of each, but financial advisors get paid in two ways: commission or fees. There are valid arguments in favor of each method.

The Arguments for Fee Based

- It is possible for an advisor to do transactions in order to generate transaction income. If the advisor is paid on a fee basis, the investor knows that the advisor has no incentive to do unnecessary transactions.
- A fee arrangement that is based on a percentage of the client's assets aligns the interest of the advisor with the interest of the client. The advisor in incented to increase the value of the client's assets because his/her fee is a percentage of the client's assets.
- The advisor monitors the client's portfolio regardless of whether there is any need to do transactions. A fee based arrangement allows the advisor to be paid fairly for that work.

The Arguments for Commission Based

- If you are a long term investor, the amount of change in the portfolio in any given year, at least after the initial portfolio is set, should be minimal. So a transaction based arrangement should cost you significantly less in the long run than a fee based arrangement.
- If you believe the advisor would do unnecessary transactions they should find another advisor. The relationship should be based on trust, and assuming lack of trust as the basis for the relationship makes no sense

So What's the Best Deal?

There is no universal answer. Some advisors only work on a fee basis, so if you want to work with that advisor you have to accept a fee arrangement. Others will give you a choice.

If you go with a fee basis, the percentage is very important because your yield on the portfolio is directly reduced by the amount of the fee. Fees generally range from 1% to 2.5%. There also may be additional charges called "ticket charges" which the advisor's firm may require you to pay. These charges may or may not be included in the fee. If an advisor is charging more than 1% not including the ticket charges or more than 1.5% including the ticket charges, then you need to ask some pretty hard questions about what the added value is. Also, if you do a fee based arrangement, make sure the 12(b)1 fees and the spreads on bonds (the difference between retail and wholesale price) are credited back to your account.

Chapter 14: Your To-Do List

If you have decided to build your own portfolio, here's your to-do list:

1. **Define your goals**

Be sure to use the S.M.A.R.T. criteria so you can figure out how much you need and you how long you have to accumulate the rest. There should not be more than *three or four goals at the most*. If there are more than that, try to combine some of them.

2. **Figure out how much you have already accumulated toward each goal**

Keep separate accounts for each goal. You may have to do some prioritizing if you don't have enough to meet all of the goals. Of course, if there is only one, such as retirement, the plan will be much simpler.

3. **Given the time you have to achieve each goal, figure out how much money you will have to contribute each year toward each goal.**

You may have to do several iterations until you settle on an amount you can contribute that will still allow you to meet your other obligations. Also, allow some money for fun. If you create a plan that makes you feel deprived you are much more likely to give up on the plan before you achieve your goals.

4. **Calculate the rates of return required to achieve the goals given the amounts you can contribute.**

This can be a little complicated, but you can find some calculators on the web that will let you approximate the rate of return. Again you may have to do some iterations until you get rates that are realistic. Be careful and realistic. Anything over 7% for a whole portfolio may require more risk than you should take.

5. **Design a portfolio to meet implement your plan.**

Using the principles outlined in Chapter 10 decide on an allocation strategy. Then put together a package of equities and fixed income investments as a model portfolio. You might want to set long term goals for the equity and fixed income portions of the portfolio such as, say, 8% for equities and 4% for fixed income. Remember *these are in no way guarantees or predictions*. They are just numbers to plug into a model based on history. If your required rate of return is higher, you will need more equities and if it is lower, you can have more fixed income.

6. **Stress test your model portfolio.**

Again, using the principles from Chapter 10, run the "stress tests" to see if you can handle the downsides. Adjust as needed until you are comfortable with the results.

7. **Commit to monitoring the portfolio no less than quarterly but no more than monthly.**

You want to stay on top of your investments, but you don't want to drive yourself crazy reacting to every short term bump in the road. Remember, several times during your investment period bad things will happen. That means you investments will lose value in some periods. Historically about one out of three years is negative. As for individual equities, set one of the computer services to alert you when there is significant news about an investment you own. When you see bad news, don't panic. Think through whether the set back is likely to be temporary or permanent based on what caused it. Think back to Warren buffet's saying, "Be fearful when everyone else is greedy and greedy when everyone else is fearful." On the other had there are times to cut your losses. If you had owned BP when they had the oil spill and you were five years from your goal you might have wanted to get out ASAP and find a better alternative.

8. **Reallocate back to your original allocation twice a year or when there has been a substantial rise or drop in the market.**

As the market has its way with your portfolio, your carefully designed portfolio will no longer match the percentages in your model. So you will need to adjust by selling some of what has gone up and buying some of what has gone down. This is called "rebalancing". (Rebalancing does not assure that you will make a profit or be protected against losses.)

In the long run even big drops in the market can be opportunities. For example, in early 2009 stocks presented a great buying opportunity. Of course, past performance is not a guarantee of future results.

9. Live your life and enjoy it.

Money is a MEANS not an END. If you have done the best you can to develop a strategy and implement it diligently, then you have done what you can. You can only do what you can do. One of the goals is always to be able to relax a little and enjoy life.

Good Luck!!

Acknowledgements

Many people have made significant contributions to the writing of this book, some of whom I have never met. Very little of the thought in the book is original. In particular I would like to acknowledge the work of Benoit Mandelbrot, Nassim Nicholas Taleb, and James Montier. The extent to which their books are quoted is testimony to how much I leaned on their thoughts.

I want to thank Dean Edell and Steve Pizzo, who have been down this authorship road ahead of me, for their encouragement and valuable suggestions. They made a difference.

My favorite English professor, Karen Ruzak, pored through the manuscript and kept my grammar and usage at an acceptable level. She compensated no little bit for my tendency to fall occasionally into prose that becomes dense and less accessible. I am grateful.

I would like to thank my muse, best friend, and primary editor – my wife Sandra Maresca. The many times she sent me back marked up manuscripts with the word "jargon" in the margin have made the book much more accessible than it might otherwise have been.

And finally, I would like to thank my clients who have trusted me with their life savings. I am honored and humbled by their trust and confidence.

About the Author

Jim Maresca brings a down-to-earth, holistic approach to the complex and challenging world of financial planning and investing. During the 45 years of his previous 5 careers (Catholic priest, political consultant, behavioral science and statistics professor, venture capitalist, and technology company management) he acquired the breadth and depth of experience for his current financial management practice. His firm, Maresca Money Management, LLC, is located in California wine country. He also hosts a weekly radio show, "Your Money and Your Life: The Dough Show." He and his artist wife, Sandra, have three grown children and live and work in the Russian River town of Guerneville. In addition to his professional practice, Jim is an elected member of the local hospital district board, serves on the board of a non-profit agency, plays third base for a men's senior hardball team, and acts in local community theatre productions.

Jim Maresca is a Registered Representative with, and securities and advisory services are offered through, LPL Financial, a Registered Investment Advisor. Member FINRA/SIPC.

www.ingramcontent.com/pod-product-compliance
Lightning Source LLC
Chambersburg PA
CBHW051345170526
45166CB00002B/959

* 9 7 8 1 4 7 7 5 1 3 4 1 5 *